Rise to Riches

Library of Congress Control Number:	2014940465
ISBN: Hardcover	978-1-4828-9970-2
Softcover	978-1-4828-9969-6
eBook	978-1-4828-9976-4

Disclaimer of Warranty/Limit of Liability
The author or publisher disclaim any responsibility for liability, loss or risk, personal or financial or otherwise that are incurred as a consequence, whether directly or indirectly, of the use and application of any of the contents of this book. The content and information in this book are to guide the reader for personal development purposes only. Even though all the stories in this book are based on real life experiences, some situations have been changed and modified for the sake of privacy and educational purposes. Some of the characters in this book are fictional. Any similarity to anyone is unintentional and coincidental.

Because of the dynamic nature of the Internet, any web addresses or links contained in this book may have changed since publication and may no longer be valid. The views expressed in this work are solely those of the author and do not necessarily reflect the views of the publisher, and the publisher hereby disclaims any responsibility for them.

To order additional copies of this book, contact
Toll Free 800 101 2657 (Singapore)
Toll Free 1 800 81 7340 (Malaysia)
orders.singapore@partridgepublishing.com

www.partridgepublishing.com/singapore

Rise to Riches

IT'S YOUR BIRTHRIGHT!

Unveil!
How to be Rich, Super Rich
with the Consciousness of our Divine Universe

Paramjit Kaur

PARTRIDGE
A Penguin Random House Company

My Intention for you

May you receive all the infinite riches of this Divine Universe.
It is your birthright!

CONTENTS

Editor's Preface

$\mathcal{P}$aramjit Kaur is one of those rare people who have experienced God in a deeply personal way, and she startles us with her enthusiastic response to God's love. Paramjit shouts with a smile, *God is wonderful!* Paramjit rejoices in God's loving kindness and shows us in refreshing terms how to have a similar experience.

Paramjit stands proudly in a long tradition of positive thinkers, while being distinct and clear in her method. Readers will benefit from her relentlessly charismatic positive attitude. What a wonderful place the world would be if we were guided by the peace and love that Paramjit gently teaches us to embrace.

This is a devotional book that shares powerful characteristics with classic spirituality. Paramjit's style is concise, but spiritually nourishing, motivational and inspiring. She expresses her message with masterful fluidity and the mantras are effective in guiding the reader to transform their understanding of God's goodness and provision.

My hope for this book is for readers to embrace the positive message and deeply experience oneness with the Divine Universe. All of us are called to follow that path. Paramjit helps us to realize its fullest potential.

Nathan J. Barnes, PhD
Fort Worth, TX
April 2013

Author's Preface

The one belief that made me take a serious and sincere effort to work on this book is the belief that no one should ever experience shortage or scarcity. Our Divine Universe is overflowing with unlimited riches and everyone is entitled to them abundantly.

This life-changing book was written after my friends insisted that I share my knowledge on manifesting riches with the consciousness of our Divine Universe, information that is too valuable to keep to myself.

I do not take credit entirely for the development of this book. God is the source; God unveils the wisdoms, truths, principles, ideas and opportunities through the mind. I am merely a humble instrument who puts pen to paper in the service of God.

My deepest gratitude to this Divine Universe, and my deepest gratitude to our LOVING GOD who is blessing everyone of us with all its infinite riches. My deepest gratitude to our loving Guardian Angels, Masters of Divine Light and Divine Love.

Blessings of super riches to the editors of this book, Andal Krishnan, Sandhya Valecha, Dr Nathan J. Barnes for making this book more understandable to the readers.

This groundbreaking book is also enriched with the wisdom of various sacred scriptures, prosperity books and my own years of experience and observations of the success of others.

With Divine Light and Love,

Paramjit Kaur

Introduction

You are meant to have unlimited riches of this Divine Universe—the finest luxuries, the ability to travel to the most exotic locations, the most fulfilling career, the best education, the finest clothes, luxurious homes and cars and loving relationships. You are not here on this divine planet earth to struggle and have worries and fears. Your life is meant to be filled with the joy and abundance of riches. This is your birthright.

The goal of this book is to eliminate the distance between your desires and the divine infinite mind, or in other words, the consciousness of our Divine Universe, which is also the consciousness of our most loving God. Remove old, negative beliefs about money and heal your relationship with money. Turbo charge your inner mental blueprint and increase your life force energy to manifest riches. Infinite riches will begin to flow in abundance and you will wonder where these riches were hiding all these years!

Do not doubt the truths and principles in this book because of their simplicity! They are the consciousness of our Divine Universe that have helped me discover my wealth, and sail to uncharted lands and undiscovered territories of infinite riches, and I am sharing these spiritual truths with you right now.

All the mantras in this book are so powerful that you will develop an aura of wealth that acts as a magnet for your desires. When you say or read these mantras with full emotion, you will start vibrating at a higher frequency, which creates magnetism and thus starts drawing towards you all the infinite riches that you desire.

I now invite you to continue reading:

How to Become Rich, Super Rich with the Consciousness of Our Divine Universe.

Rise to Riches. IT is you birthright!

With Divine Light and Love,

Paramjit Kaur

CHAPTER 1

Rise to Riches
With The Consciousness of
Our Divine Universe

"The source of all can only respond with what it is, and what the Universe is, it is an infinite supply. It can't relate to scarcity, or things not working out, because it's none of these things."

Dr. Wayne W. Dyer
The Power of Intention

What is the nature of our Divine Universe?

Our Divine Universe is a limitless storehouse of riches beyond our wildest imagination; more accurately, it is the source of UNLIMITED RICHES.

Our Divine Universe is a constantly evolving, expanding, loving, creative organism. Evidence of this is all around us.

Look at the *unlimited bounty, diversity and perfect harmony of Nature!*

Look at the *advancement and breakthroughs in technologies!*

Look at the *unlimited wealth in our relationships, our health, our knowledge, our wisdom, the things we have and the things we have experienced!*

These are all UNLIMITED RICHES!

Wisdom from the Indian spiritual text of *Upanishads,* so eloquently says:

> *"All this is full, all that is full. From the fullness, fullness comes. When fullness is taken from fullness, fullness still remains."*

The consciousness of our Divine Universe is an eternal spring that knows no limits. Our Divine Universe is prosperous, affluent and unlimited in its creativity.

The unlimited abundance of our Divine Universe is *available to all.* It is in a constant state of manifesting and supplying the desires, wishes and dreams of everyone. It is continuously giving unlimited prosperity to all without playing favorites; no desires are denied.

The Divine Universe knows no bound to giving. It does not know scarcity or shortage; it only knows unlimited abundance, creation, unconditional giving, and it never stops giving.

It never says, "I don't think that's possible!" or "There's not enough to go around!"

The wealth of our Divine Universe is never depleted. Tune in to your loving God's frequency and you will know beyond any and all doubt that your loving God, the universal mind, and the Divine Universe of your loving God is UNLIMITED CONSCIOUSNESS.

Align with the Unlimited Consciousness of our Divine Universe

Aligning with the unlimited consciousness of our Divine Universe means that you move beyond hoarding, selfishness, and greed. Hoarding, selfishness, and greed are against the consciousness of our Divine Universe.

Every soul's true nature is unlimited abundance and affluence! There are endless opportunities for creating wealth. If you ever have thoughts or feelings of stinginess, selfishness or hoarding, immediately look at the evidence for ever-flowing generosity in our Divine Universe.

For example, the sun is radiating its most beautiful sunlight on everyone, not only a selected few. The trees and plants are all sharing their flowers, fruits, and fragrances with all of God's creatures. The rain showers and cleanses everyone and everything. This loving unconditional sharing is without any expectations! Our Divine Universe is beautiful and abundant in its gifts to us. The unlimited riches of the Divine Universe "BELONG TO ALL."

Let go of the need to hoard and accept that the Universe is inherently generous and that at every moment, it creates wonderful things for all of us everywhere, filling all vessels, pots, purses, pockets and domains.

Let go of the negative beliefs that resources are scarce, opportunities are limited. Become aware that nothing is lost; nothing can be taken away from you.

Align with the unlimited consciousness of our Divine Universe; think like a creator with unlimited resources to draw upon.

Never again say the words, "poverty, poor or limited." It is not the consciousness of our Divine Universe and it is not your natural state as YOU ARE THE OFFSPRING of this rich Divine Universe!

Poverty is a conditioned state that has been imposed on you by your thoughts of fear, lack and unworthiness.

We are taught that competition and struggle are necessary components to life. This is a flawed premise. The truth is that to manifest riches is to align with the unlimited consciousness of our Divine Universe. There is no such concept as poverty, limitedness or lack in the divine consciousness.

Turbo-charge your mindset with statements that express:

☆ *Unlimited*
☆ *Plenty*
☆ *Millions, Billions, Trillions*
☆ *Wealthy*
☆ *Abundance*
☆ *Affluence*
☆ *Riches, Super Riches*

All statements that carry these ideas will align you with the consciousness of our Divine Universe. Stubbornly deny that lack has any place or reality in your life. It does not!

We all have a choice to make. We can choose to be wealthy or poor, successful or unsuccessful, happy or miserable. Choose to be wealthy, healthy, successful and happy, *now*! *It is your birthright as you are the offspring of our Divine Universe.*

Impress these thoughts onto your subconscious mind and forever eliminate negative thoughts that keep you in mediocrity and lack. The Divine Universe will then assist you in achieving every dream you have, including wealth and a life of full expression and potential!

✯ With a smile, declare the following mantra. Your divine loving God will bring forth all your heart's desires to you effortlessly:

"I am God's Divine Offspring and I think the way God thinks. I can create anything I desire. I am ever-expanding, unlimited, creative and boundless. I joyfully live my purpose.

I bless and radiate unlimited divine light, love and prosperity for all. My horizons are unlimited; and my riches are unlimited.

My resources come to me through many channels and I am receiving unlimited money, wealth, wisdom, knowledge and ideas.

I harmoniously align with the unlimited consciousness of my loving God, who is the divine source of all unlimited riches."

CHAPTER 2

Your Desires for Riches
Are Divine Impulses

"Desire that which you desire, and desire with all the power of mind and soul. We invariably receive what we desire, no more no less."

Christian Larson
The Path to Roses

If you have a desire to be wealthy, you may be surprised to learn that this desire is a divine impulse and that this divine impulse is the starting point of your journey to wealth.

Judge Thomas Troward, influential figure in the science of the mind, in his *Edinburgh Lecture* (1917) said, *"Desires are divine impulses which stimulate us to growth and constant development. The omnipotence of the Supreme Intelligence is absolutely unlimited. It wants you to have everything you desire."*

If you believe this to be true, you may ask this great question:

"If God wants us to have everything that we desire, then why are some desires not manifested?"

You may also ask:

"Why does it sometimes take a long time to get what we want?"

Your desires are divine impulses, but impulses in and of themselves are not enough to bring your desires into manifestation. In order to manifest your desires, they must be in vibrational harmony with the consciousness of our Divine Universe.

Know the Essence of Your Desire

To transform your desires to manifestation, the first step is to ask yourself, "What is the true motivation of my desire? Are my desires crystal clear? Am I being specific?"

Saying, "I want to be rich," "I want to have money," is the starting point, but at this point it's nothing more than vague hope!

Merely generalizing does not magnetize results. Make your desires as clear and as specific as you can. Ask yourself the following questions:

☆ *What is my desire going to do for me?*
☆ *What is the real purpose of that desire?*
☆ *What reason do I have for wanting something?*
☆ *How would I feel owning it?*

7

Consider the times you desperately wanted something only to get it and still feel a sense of disappointment because you thought it would fulfill some deeper need, but it did not.

Pioneer of the self-help movement, Wallace D. Wattles, wrote in his book *The Science of Getting Rich*, *"You must now ask what you want and be specific and definite. You can never get rich or start the creative process into action by sending out unformed longings and vague desires."* How true!

Manifesting our desires requires knowing the essence of what we want. But why is it so important to be specific and know the essence of our desires?

Let's illustrate with an example. Say you want a new house. You have been told to visualize the house in great detail and, yes, you must do that.

However, add another dimension to this by creating a Statement of Desire describing clearly the essence of what you want.

Use the following points as your guide:

1. Develop a vivid picture of what this new house is going to do for you, the way this particular structure and location would fulfill your needs and wants. How does this new house make you feel? This is the most critical aspect of any desire, knowing the underlying reason for wanting it in the first place.

2. Visualize specifics, but make sure they address your reasons.

    ✭ *Do you want peaceful, serene views of the countryside? Why is this important to you?*

⭐ *Do you want a vibrant, lively neighborhood? Why is this important to you?*

⭐ *Do you want a place that allows you to express your creativity or entertain large groups of friends? Why is this important to you?*

⭐ *What specific functions of the house are important to you, and why? What inner longings would be satisfied by those functions?*

3. At this point, you should be clear about certain architectural features of your dream house, but be open to the unexpected. It may be that the perfect house for you is not in the exact location you imagined or even in the same architectural style.

You can apply these same guidelines to any desire. If you have trouble answering these questions, i.e., naming a particular feature you desire, but not being able to answer why you want it, then you are not clear enough on your desire.

Crystallize it in your mind first and see if it addresses your inner longing; if it does not, the desire may not be worth pursuing!

As you become familiar with the essence of your desire, you will see that you suddenly have options.

Perhaps the thing you wished for is the perfect way to satisfy your ultimate need and perhaps you will discover that something else addresses your needs even better! Address the 'why' and you have uncovered the essence of the thing you want! You have tapped into your subconscious mind and are on the way to creating your reality.

Another example is the classic, "I want plenty of money!"

This desire for plenty of money is not clear enough to manifest your money!

What is 'plenty'? Define 'plenty'.

'Plenty' to one person is different from 'plenty' to another. You have to be specific as to the amount you want and the definite date you wish to have it. You must also be specific about 'why' you want that amount.

What do you want to do with that *amount of money*—perhaps travel, buy nice things, pay for a university education, give to charity? Visualize how your money can make you feel happy and satisfied. That is the essence of your desire for money!

Burning Desire with Burning Faith

New Thought leader and author of *The Path to Roses*, Christian Larson, brilliantly said: *"A desire with a burning faith is the starting point from which the dreamer must take off. Faith takes mind and soul into the greater realms of life. It goes upon the boundless and awakens those interior spiritual forces that have the power to do anything. This is why all things become possible when we have faith."* Well said!

What does it mean to have 'Burning Desire with Burning Faith'?

How do you magnetize your 'Burning Desire' with 'Burning Faith'?

'Burning Desire with Burning Faith' creates a magnetic pull between you and your goal and the feeling is powerfully irresistible!

Miracles occur when your desire becomes most intense, when you feel that your desire has set you afire. When you combine burning desire with burning faith, there is no obstacle that cannot be overcome!

'Burning Desire with Burning Faith' knows no limitations or doubt.

If you study people who have rose to riches, super riches, you will always reach the same conclusion: they have burning desires with burning faith. It is the dominant factor in any successful endeavor.

Think of all the successes, achievements, breakthroughs, and marvelous inventions that have come about because of burning desire with burning faith. Legendary Thomas Edison, despite failing 1,000 times, created the light bulb.

Other examples abound. Henry Ford, a school dropout, produced affordable cars. Technopreneur Steve Jobs, founder of Apple, built a business empire by creating the most user-friendly computers in the world.

If your dominant desire is to be wealthy, back it up with 'Burning Desire with Burning Faith', which means having complete trust in your manifesting power and in your divinely unlimited, generous and loving God.

Desire Proclaiming: "It Is Already Mine"

Having crystal clear burning desires with burning faith is not enough to manifest what you desire. You need to be more determined than that! A powerful way to magnetize your desires for spontaneous manifestation is claiming that, *"It is already mine."*

When you invoke such a powerful statement, you are emphatically stating, "This is what I want!"

Highly respected author, Sanaya Roman in her book *Creating Money*, said, *"The Universe responds to your positive talk. Even if you do not have something you want in your life right now. If you begin to talk and act as if you are certain you will have it, you will draw to you the circumstances to have it."* This is absolutely true!

This may not be logical to some minds. However, the miracles of manifestation start unfolding when we talk as if it has already been received.

Here is an example from my own experience: I was desperate to win a lucrative supplier contract from a multinational company. I wrote a decree saying, *"I have already won the contract, my customer is happy with my proposal and we are now prospering together."*

I read my decree daily and visualized having won the contract. Within a few months I had won the contract! I have achieved many successes by proclaiming, *"It is already mine."*

You too can get all your desires manifested into reality, but make sure your desires are not just vague desires, but burning desires with burning faith.

Our Divine Universe does not respond to a single thought, but when you hold your thought long enough, claiming that it is already yours and vibrate with strong positive emotions, your desires will manifest spontaneously.

✦ With a smile, consider this timeless wisdom of William Shakespeare:

> *"Assume a virtue if you have it not. Look the part, dress the part, and act the part. Be successful in your thought first. It won't be long before you will be successful before the world as well."*

CHAPTER 3

Stimulate Wealth With Your Inner Blueprint

> *"Why should you insult your creator by indifference or neglect in the use of his most priceless gift—the power of the mind."*
>
> *Napoleon Hill*
> *Law of Success*

Why is one brother rich and the other mediocre? Why do some businesses thrive and some shut down within a few months? Why do some people get job promotions and pay increases while their co-workers remain where they are?

Why do some people remain stagnant, no growth in their endeavors?

And why do some people continually experience the same repeated and unwanted reality?

If you have a mediocre life ask yourself, "What is preventing you to rise to riches super riches?"

The answer may not be what you want to hear, but it will be what you need to hear, that it is because of ignorance of the proper application of the most vital force.

"YOUR INNER BLUEPRINT"

Which is the combination of your thoughts, inner dialogue, inner pictures, feelings and mental belief system.

Ignorance of these applications excuses no one. Whatever your field or profession is, you must learn how to apply them. History has evidence of the rise and fall of people according to their use of thoughts and mental beliefs and it is evident that failures are transformed to success with this power.

Legendary judge and mental science writer Thomas Troward, in his lecture notes *Law and the Word* said, *"The first principle in getting rich is from your Thought Power."*

Identify with this remarkable truth explained by Troward, "This is a vibrational universe." Everything is vibrational, including your inner blueprint. You can change your imperfect life into a perfect life, from poor to rich, from sickness to health, and from depression to joy with your inner blueprint.

Mastering Your Inner Blueprint

You have just read the metaphysical truth that what you are surrounded with, what you have, what you are, where you are, the type of career you have, the success you have achieved, the opportunities you attract, your state of health, your relationships, and the status of your financial riches all correspond to your inner blueprint.

To stimulate the wealth of your birthright, you must first *"evaluate your belief system."* Your belief system must be in alignment with the abundant consciousness of our Divine Universe.

Author Sanaya Roman in her book *Creating Money* said, *"Beliefs are assumptions about the nature of reality, and because you create what you believe in, you will have many 'proofs' that reality operates the way you think it does. For instance, a person who believes that the Universe is abundant will act in such a way that he or she experiences abundance, and a person who believes that money comes only from working hard will receive money only from hard work."*

The beliefs that we hold deep within create our reality. Although sometimes it can be difficult to be aware of our beliefs, we can learn to identify them by listening to our inner dialogue.

Think of the magnificence you can create when you master your inner blueprint! When negativity is gone and joyful abundance permeates you, your outer world will begin to match the bountiful, limitless happiness you hold within.

Imagine yourself as a seed that has vast potential. Don't damage the seed that's been planted by continually poking at it with sticks of negativity!

Nurture it with love. Water it with positive belief. Nourish it with positive thoughts. And then, your seed—your true self—will blossom into a radiant, beautiful flower that delights and enriches not only you, but everyone around you.

A True Story of Negative Self-Worth

I have a friend who is highly educated and a dedicated, hard working lady. She has been working in a multinational organization for the last fifteen years, but has never been promoted. Younger colleagues who joined the company much later have been promoted to senior management. As I probed further into her career path and her belief system, I realized that she was burdened with a negative inner dialogue of her worthiness.

She wants to be promoted, but at the same time she feels that others are better than her and this is reflected in the way she speaks about herself! She subconsciously projects feelings of unworthiness and her bosses pick up on it and give her exactly what she asks for. Energetically, she is asking to be bypassed for promotion!

Her limiting belief about her lack of worthiness is deeply ingrained in her subconscious and it has held back her desires for career advancement.

In his book, *Spontaneous Fulfillment of Desire*, spiritual writer Deepak Chopra pointed out that, *"The quality of your inner dialogue is instantly obvious to other people, although it might not be recognized for what it is. When you practice positive inner dialogue, people will want to bond with you, help you and be near you. They want to share in the love, knowingness and bliss that shines through your eyes and is reflected in your every action. This is true inner power."*

"Start evaluating your inner dialogue." You may be surprised with what you learn! For example, if you grew up in an environment where you kept hearing "we can't afford that," "it's hard to come by," "we are not capable," or "everything is so hard," you have probably developed a belief that you are not meant to have things you want!

As you uncover your belief system through this introspection, make a list of all your beliefs and ask the following questions:

- ☆ *Are my beliefs serving my higher good?*
- ☆ *Are they empowering or limiting?*
- ☆ *Are they moving me forward or keeping me stagnant?*
- ☆ *Are they inviting prosperity or repelling it?*
- ☆ *Are they built based on fear?*
- ☆ *Do these fears serve my present desires?*

Limiting beliefs paralyze your actions and block the manifestation of your desires. Beliefs that you are not worthy of wealth, that you are incapable of achieving wealth, that you are not good enough, and many beliefs like these sabotage your dreams.

If your belief system is not drawing you to what you desire, take heart! You can create and rewrite new beliefs that serve your higher purpose. *Let go of those old beliefs!*

See the Divine Universe from the perspective of abundance, achievement, love, infinite possibilities and fulfillment. Let go of your attachment to seeing the world from a perspective of scarcity, struggle, lack and fear.

Become a Deliberate Creator of your life

The ability to change your inner blueprint deliberately is evident in sports. The greatest champions of sports are made because of their amazing inner blueprints. Elite athletes train their minds as diligently as they train their bodies by deliberately visualizing their desired end results; their self-talk is positive, powerful, and in alignment with their desires. Elite athletes don't let anything pollute their vision and they master their minds the same way they master their bodies.

You can train your mind like an elite athlete. When you turbo-charge your inner blueprint by deliberately desiring the end results, you will attract the right people, resources and opportunities to you, and doors will open to you.

Whatever you desire, imagine it deeply. Savor the images and emotions. Continue imagining until you feel that "*you have already received it,*" until the mental image feels as real to you as your 'normal' life.

Then, watch what happens. Remember, there must be no doubts, only faith, and you must believe you deserve this as a child of the Divine Universe!

The acceptance that you are the creator of your life is one of the most exhilarating and liberating feelings you will ever have. You get to decide what to create!

Become a deliberate creator of your life by monitoring and discriminating your thoughts, having positive inner dialogue and imagination. Every persistent thought and inner dialogue attracts another and another.

Deliberately replace all negative thoughts with happiness, prosperity and unlimited abundance. All you need or want has already been given to you in abundance in your thoughts. It is up to you to bring it into your physical reality by harmonizing with it.

You are not at the mercy of any external forces. Your Divine God has blessed you with the ability to master your mind. *Use that GIFT!*

☆ With a smile, say the following powerful mantra as often as possible and it will imprint positive beliefs into your subconscious mind and become your habitual way of thinking:

"I make a conscious decision that every thought, every word, every story, every belief, every feeling, every imagination, and every visualization that I have makes me feel good, joyful, and uplifts me at all times.

I lovingly release old beliefs that no longer serve me. I believe in my unlimited prosperity. I deserve the abundance of this prosperous Divine Universe, as it is my divine birthright."

CHAPTER 4

Manifesting Money Spontaneously

"Money is filled with the intelligence of the Universe, from which it was created. Money reacts to your attitude about it. If you think favorably about money, you multiply it. If you criticize and condemn it, your money dissipates and repels from you."

Catherine Ponder
The Dynamic Laws of Prosperity

*H*ave you been complaining that you are frugal, but money seems to dissipate and you always seem to need more?

Have you been lamenting that you toil harder than others, but you have "nothing to show for it?"

If yes, you may say that life is unfair.

Let's look at it from a different angle. Instead of complaining about life being unfair, let's look deeper than what your senses can perceive to find the root cause of your lack of financial abundance. The root cause of the lack of financial riches may arise when, thoughtlessly or unconsciously, you utter the following negative statements:

- ✮ *I have to work hard for money; money never comes easily.*
- ✮ *It is beautiful, but I can't afford it. Everything is getting so expensive.*
- ✮ *Money isn't everything! Money cannot buy happiness.*
- ✮ *The rich get richer and the poor get poorer.*
- ✮ *There is never enough money in my bank account.*
- ✮ *I have lost money in partnerships. I don't trust business partnerships anymore.*
- ✮ *The economy is getting bad and is hurting everyone.*
- ✮ *I can't stand my debtors; I dread receiving bills.*
- ✮ *My boss, my job, my home, my spouse, my kids, my cars, the government, the economy, the weather—I can tell you a hundred reasons why I'm not rich financially!*

If you have been complaining, blaming, criticizing, condemning and judging everything and everyone for your financial troubles, without realizing it, you are attracting the same vibrations that you send out!

Some people, unconsciously or ignorantly, lose promotions and pay increases as a result of negative criticizing, negative thoughts, and gossips about their work, workplace and their employers. We can't expect our employer to promote us or give us an increase in salary when we send out vibrations of disrespect and resentment. People pick up on the 'vibes' we send out. We can pretend to be positive, but our energetic vibrations don't lie!

A negative attitude toward money, employers, or the success of others makes it hard to manifest your desires. Take two people in the same business at the same location, for instance; the one who flourishes is the one with the positive beliefs about money and the one who is trapped in mediocrity has negative beliefs about money.

Most of the time, condemning or criticizing is done unconsciously. We don't mean to do it, but we end up repelling the things we want and need, such as a fulfilling career, a loving relationship, financial abundance, the comforts of life, etc. Blaming others for our miseries and failures gives away our power to change our circumstances.

Our emotions are our attracting factors. Negative or pessimistic viewpoints and beliefs about money are not in harmony with the consciousness of our Divine Universe.

If you find yourself criticizing or thinking negatively about money or anything related to your finances, for example, your career, employers, business partners and the economy of your country, ask yourself these two questions:

☆ *Do I believe this to be true?*
☆ *If so, why?*

Then deeply examine your beliefs about money. Many of them are unconsciously adopted because of things others may have said. Just imagine you had been told the opposite. What would your beliefs be? What would your outlook on life be like if your beliefs were different?

You have a choice right now to decide whether a belief you hold is true and whether it serves you. If not, change it. Adopt a new belief that is in harmony with the consciousness of our Divine Universe.

Stop Talk of Hard Times and Hardships!

Just because some people are complaining about how bad the economy is, doesn't mean there aren't riches and fortunes to be made. Do you know that some people become super rich during economic downturn? Some people become creative and inventive during hard times and these are the people whose fortunes are vast.

So! Stop talking about bad financial affairs.

Stop saying that times are bad.

You are doing an injustice to your employer and your country with such negative talks. Always say, *"Times are really good for me, and improving every day!"*

Never utter your shortcomings, fears or doubts! Delete 'hardships' from your vocabulary! Do not speak negatively, even if your present circumstances are negative.

Stop gloating over the financial hardships of others as this is exactly what you will attract. Do not even speak when you are in a bad mood, as the negative vibration you send out could lead to confrontation and repercussions you can't possibly imagine.

Never utter words that discourage others or create unhappiness in others because that negativity will bounce back to you. *Always utter words that bring joy to every heart, as this joy will boomerang back to you!*

Just like farmers who choose their seed with great care to grow healthy crops, in the same manner we have to intelligently choose our words. Our words bring forth the kind of crop we plant; we become what we say or in other words, we reap what we sow!

Legendary Unity Church Minister, Charles Fillmore, founder of the Unity Church (1854) and author of the book called *Prosper* advises:

> *"If your purse seems empty, deny the lack and say, 'You are filled even now with the bounty of God, my Father, who supplies all my wants. If your rooms are empty, deny the appearance and determine that prosperity is manifest in every part of every room. Never think of yourself as poor or needy.*
>
> *Do not talk about hard times or the necessity for strict economy. Even 'the walls have ears' and unfortunately, memories too. Do not think how little you have, but how much you have.*
>
> *Turn only those words that charge the home atmosphere with the idea of plenty, for life attracts like in the unseen, as well as the seen. Fill your home with the thoughts and words of plenty, of love and of God's substance."*

Take heed of the above wisdom of Charles Fillmore.

Never ever, under any circumstances, utter what you don't want to come to you!

Talk of hard times, poverty and famine are not the consciousness of our Divine Universe and has no place in the mind of our loving Divine God. In mind and in spirit there are only unlimited riches. Avoid talking of hard times and replace it with talk of abundance and riches.

Love, Respect and Bless Your Money

Never criticize your financial related endeavors such as your money, wealth, wealthy people and their wealth. You want what's good, so if you say money is bad and rich people are bad and yet you desire wealth, you are contradicting yourself.

Money is an energy that flows like a river. It flows to people who have a positive attitude about money. It dissipates or never flows to those who have negative beliefs about money. *Money is a divine channel between you and your desires. Money is there for you to exchange for all your needs and desires.*

Your inner speech is the cause of your life experiences. If you want to attract inexhaustible financial riches, make sure your inner speech is the same as your desires. Affirm the following three powerful spontaneous money manifestation mantras, as it will open the doors to super financial abundance.

Mantra1. What you love will always seek you. Love having abundance of money. Imagine receiving abundance of money. The more you picture receiving abundance of money, the more you attract it.

✰ Smile and joyfully say:

> *"I love having plenty of money flowing to me. I bless all the money of my country and I bless all the money of other countries. I lovingly open my divine hands to receive the ever-flowing abundance of money. Plenty of money is flowing to me every moment. I love my money and bless my money."*

Mantra2. If you desire something, but have no means to purchase it in the present moment, do not ever accept that you can't afford it.

☆ Smile and joyfully say:

> *"I would love to have (your desire). It belongs to me. My divine loving God will make sure that I have it. God is my ever present help. I bless all the riches of my most loving and generous divine God. All the riches of my loving God are circulating abundantly in my life right now."*

Mantra 3. If you see others having all the wonderful things in their life, do not get jealous or start comparing and harboring ill thoughts. Comparing your riches with someone who has more than you creates a feeling of lack. It blocks the flow of riches. Instead, bless and rejoice in the riches of others. When you bless and rejoice in the riches of others, you attract the same.

☆ Smile and joyfully say:

> *"I rejoice, bless, and radiate divine light to the riches of others. And I deserve it, too. It is my turn, now; our Divine Universe is already manifesting that which I rejoice in others."*

CHAPTER **5**

Our Role as Debtor and Creditor For a Prosperous Life

"It is not only unpleasant and unnecessary, but foolish and dangerous to waste time and energy criticizing anything, especially, financial obligations owed or owing you."

Catherine Ponder
The Dynamic Laws of Prosperity

In this capitalist society, all of us play the role of debtors and creditors alternatively. When someone owes us and does not pay us back or delays payment, we whine, "My debtors are not paying me and they are avoiding me."

When we owe others, we whine. "I can't pay my debts on time. I can't afford to pay, creditors are chasing me. I am in arrears. I hate receiving outstanding payment notices. I hate going through credit card statements".

Little do we realize that not only does negative whining create stress and drain our energy; moreover, negative whining and complaining about debtors and creditors or people who we are dealing with financially, creates a negative vibrational relationship. And our debtors and creditors can subconsciously sense these negative vibrations.

Catherine Ponder in her book, *The Dynamic Laws of Prosperity*, wisely said, *"The technique of getting debts paid—both those you owe and those who owe you—is first an inner work in the realm of mental attitude. Others can be so repelled by your critical, unforgiving, condemnatory thoughts that they shrink from wanting to pay you what is owed."*

If this sounds like you, evaluate if you have been consciously, unconsciously, or ignorantly thinking or speaking badly about your creditors or debtors.

Believe it, this negative energy is the cause of resistance to your flow of money. Your negative emotions about debtors and creditors offer negative vibrational frequencies, which are not in harmony with the consciousness of our Divine Universe.

Paying Your Debt Joyfully

If you are a debtor, never say, "I can't afford to pay," or "I won't pay." Never defame or speak ill of your creditors or their products and services without constructive evaluation or justification. If you are not happy with your creditors, reason out with them directly. Always think well and speak well of your creditors.

When you receive bills, do not dread them. It is your responsibility to settle the bills; don't forget, you have received and benefited from your creditors' products and services. Each time you send your money out, be happy that it is contributing to the riches of others.

As you make your payment to your creditors, joyfully bless all your payments and bless the receivers of your payments to prosper abundantly!

When you send your money with blessings, gratitude, and love, imagine joyfully that more is coming to you, and you open more doors for the universal flow of money.

When you have the thought "I can't pay my bills," reverse it and with a smile, affirm this powerful mantra:

> *"All my bills are paid immediately. I pay my debts joyfully in an honest and timely manner. As I pay my debts, I bless my creditors and their riches.*
>
> *I declare abundant of riches for all my creditors. May their riches multiply abundantly. And may we continue to have good relationships for our continuing prosperity.*
>
> *I bless the money and checks I give to my creditors. My most loving and generous God is the provider of my riches. All my riches are increasing superlatively."*

This change might not happen overnight! It takes persistent, consistent affirmations and faith to change your positive beliefs about money.

Trust in the journey!

Getting Your Debtors to Pay

Some of us do not get paid by our debtors because mentally we are harassing them with all kinds of negative thoughts such as he or she is dishonest by not paying us back. Avoid thoughts and speeches that your debtors are not paying you.

Just because your debtors delay their payment does not mean that they do not intend to pay you. It is a crime to accuse them of dishonesty without giving them a chance to work out some sort of agreement.

More often than not, people are embarrassed and ashamed that they don't have the means to pay you. Do not add to that negativity by implanting your own angry thoughts. Always think and speak well of those who owe you.

If you negatively lament about who owes you or who is not paying you, this is what you will continue to attract.

A True Story about Loaning Money

A friend complained that she loaned her friend $150,000 of her savings and the latter did not seem to be inclined to pay her back. This woman displayed continuous bitterness and resentment towards her friend, lamenting, "I valued her friendship and gave her my savings and she is not honoring her words and friendship."

I told her that the cure to this problem was to first and foremost remove all resentment towards her friend from her thoughts. She tried initially, but could not as her anger was overpowering her. I told her to try again when she was in a relaxed state. I advised her to radiate divine love, peace, light and bless her friend with all the infinite riches, and to shower her friend with compassionate thoughts.

I also advised that she should stop saying that her friend was not paying her back. Her inner talk had to change immediately. I told her to stop any doubt or negativity against her friend and I gave her the following simple but powerful mantra:

> *"My friend (name of the friend) is paying back my money. I bless my friend with divine love, peace, light and joy. Wealth of the infinite is flowing to my friend (name of the friend) right now.*
>
> *Our most loving God is prospering my friend with abundance of money. I bless the riches, which God is providing my friend. I thank and bless my friend for paying me back and I thank my loving God for prospering her."*

This friend of mine repeated the above powerful mantra several times a day. She visualized that her friend was paying back the money and she was holding the money and depositing the money in her bank account.

Guess what happened!

Less than 3 months later, her friend contacted her to pay her back and apologized for the delay.

Compassionate Thoughts towards your Debtors

Your debtors may be late in paying you. Instead of getting angry with them, have compassionate thoughts toward your debtors and wish them abundance of riches. When you radiate compassionate thoughts, your relationship with money and your relationship with those who borrow from you also changes.

Believe me! This vibration will create the flow toward you. And those who owe you will pay you in no time.

Whenever you have thoughts that your debtors or friends are not paying you what they owe you, reverse it and affirm the following mantra:

✮ Smile and joyfully say:

"I trust my debtor (name of the debtor) because he or she is a child of this Divine Universe of abundance.

Lovingly I radiate divine light and divine love to my debtor and all his/her endeavors. My Divine Universe is prospering my debtor so that my debtor pays his/her debts."

CHAPTER **6**

Riches with Unconditional Princely Kindness

"The living of life consists in continuously increasing life; there is no other way to live."

Wallace D. Wattles
The Science of Getting Rich

We live in a beautiful Divine Universe which is filled with a beautiful exchange of harmonious energy and a beautifully balanced symphony of unconditional princely kindness in the form of giving and receiving, loving and being loved, serving and prospering.

This exchange of harmonious energy teaches us the workings of the universal laws by demonstrating its powerful divine Law of Increase. Essentially everything in our Divine Universe is about increase, growth and expansion. It is the consciousness of our Divine Universe. From a single plant comes many and from each of those, many more. From a single idea, many more follow.

The most powerful metaphor of how the Divine Universe is ever-expanding is the fruits we eat. One fruit contains many seeds and from each seed a tree can grow, and each tree produces many thousands of its fruits in its lifetime. Each seed from a fruit can grow into another tree, so there is no limit to the possible number of trees that can come from a single seed!

Similarly, the flame of a single candle can light an infinite number of candles. A single thought can create many more like it and gains strength as it multiplies. It is the same with money. A single coin, used wisely, can become a vast fortune.

As a way to multiply our riches, all great spiritual texts, as well as the great spiritual teachers such as Buddha, Guru Nanak, Jesus Christ, Lao-Tzu, the Sufis and the Rishis, teach us that we need to align with the 'princely kindnesses' of our Divine.

Unconditional Princely Kindness
"The Guru Nanak Way"

A great sage called Guru Nanak (1469) founder of Sikhism, made an impact in the hearts of many in the fellowship of unconditional princely kindness.

Guru Nanak was disturbed by the political chaos and religious oppression that had caused hunger and misery to the people around him. To handle this, he embarked on a journey of higher consciousness in the form of establishing the concept of *'Langar Vand Ke Shakko'*, which means equal distribution of food where rich and poor, males and females, of high caste and low caste, kings and beggars, irrespective of race and religion, could sit and eat the same food together. Guru Nanak set up community kitchens in all Gurdwaras and Sikh centers.

This distribution system developed a sense of caring in the community and changed the attitudes of people regarding status, thus, developing compassion for one another, as well as encouraging the giving of oneself to serve the community.

Today, these community kitchens are found throughout the world in all Sikh Gurdwaras and also in Sikh homes.

This divine virtue; it is a guide for all of us to look into the wisdom of unconditional giving and sharing in a community. Guru Nanak said that in order to serve the Creator, we must first serve the created!

Unconditional serving, sharing and giving is a divine princely kindness. The more you give, serve and share unconditionally, the more you open up to bliss, peace, joy and love. It removes scarcity, blesses the giver, and each gift is a seed whose expanded bounty you will reap.

Unconditional Princely Kindness should be rendered gracefully, joyfully and willingly with no expectation of reward. It must create happiness for the giver and for the receiver. Giving grudgingly has negative energy in it and negative energy blocks the flow of infinite riches. *When you give unconditionally and joyfully, your returns multiply.*

Giving should not be limited to money or material things; it involves aligning the receiver with their higher purpose. Do or give anything you can give to enrich the lives of others. If you teach someone a new skill, your gift transcends the immediate need and helps a person grow. If you give knowledge, your gift enables the receiver to enrich and expand his or her life much more than if you simply complete a task for them and do not impart the knowledge of how to do it.

The gift might be material, or non-material. It may be words of appreciation, compliments, flowers, blessings or prayers, food, clothes, money, or education scholarships.

When your giving is for the benefit of others, you create a golden aura of riches and you set into motion a spontaneous, effortless, and miraculous turning point in your life. Giving love brings love. Giving understanding brings understanding. Giving services and talents increases and multiplies prosperity.

Acts of unconditional princely kindness signal our Divine Universe that you are open to more abundance, and our Divine Universe will set the flow of abundance in motion toward you. Recognize the universal scope of this law, and then the gift you bestow has a chance to go out and to come back multiplied.

It is unimaginable how far blessings travel around our Divine Universe before they return back. It is an encouraging fact that the longer the blessings take in returning, the more divine hands they are passing through and the more divine hearts they are touching. All these hands and hearts add something to the blessings in substance. They are increased all the more when they do return.

With a smile, make a commitment that every moment, wherever you are, whomever you meet, you will bring gifts of princely kindness in the form of silently saying:

"May I help, May I serve, May I give, May I bless you, May I reach out and touch others, May I elevate every ordinary moment to a delightful moment."

CHAPTER 7

Stop Saying "No Thanks" Open your hands to Receiving

"Each day offers us the gift of being a special occasion if we can simply learn that as well as giving, it is blessed to receive with grace and a grateful heart!"
Sarah Ban Breathnach
Simple Abundance

S*ome* people pray for riches, love and healthy relationships and talk about their dreams and desires, yet when love, praise, opportunities, favors and compliments, money, ideas, gifts come to them they refuse them by uttering:

☆ *No Thanks! or No Thank You!*
☆ *I am not worthy to receive it!*
☆ *It's too good for me!*
☆ *This is too good to be true!*
☆ *I don't deserve it!*

This is said with kind intentions of not burdening or imposing on the giver, but such refusal not only blocks the blessings of the giver and receiver but also blocks the circulation of giving and receiving.

Laurence G. Bolt in his popular book *The Tao of Abundance* said: *"Though we tend to underrate its value, our ability to receive is as important as our ability to give. In fact, we can only give to others what we are willing to receive for ourselves. Receive and you must give: this is a spiritual law of the Universe."*

Respected Channel for Orin and author of *Creating Money*, Sanaya Roman said: *"The more you open to receive, the more you can give. Receive money from people, receive the form and substance of what they give you and do so with warmth and graciousness."*

I absolutely agree with respected authors Laurence G. Bolt and Sanaya Roman that *"Receiving is as paramount as giving."*

There can be no giving without receiving. We must balance giving and receiving equally in order to draw riches to ourselves. The principle of giving and receiving is the most powerful *"Spiritual Law"* of our Divine Universe!

You give someone the joy that comes from giving something to you! Then you open yourself up to joyfully receiving all of *God's Divine Gifts!*

My Experience with the 'Principle of Giving and Receiving'

Being a most generous soul I was always giving, but I was not receiving my good that I deserved. I was curious to find the truth and started to research the universal 'Laws of Riches'. I learnt this Divine Law from my favorite prosperity author, Catherine Ponder. I am grateful for her knowledge and I would like to share with you her wisdom:

> *"If you are one of those people who has also believed it isn't nice to expect to receive, though you have given generously to life, then you can know this: All giving you have done over the years has built up in the invisible a tremendous backlog of good for you to receive. That accumulated good has remained in the invisible, simply because you have not expected to receive and have not known how to open your mind to the idea of receiving that good. You can now begin to receive your rich dividends which have accumulated from all your previous giving simply by saying daily to yourself:*
>
> *"I am receiving; I am receiving all the goods God wants to give me. I have been giving, giving, giving. I now balance that giving by being willing to receive, receive, and receive all the good that has been accumulating for me. I have given richly and I am receiving richly, now."*

After comprehending this wisdom of Catherine Ponder, I realized that I was only invoking the 'Principle of Giving!' I told myself I had to open my mind to the 'Principle of Receiving.'

It was great to know I was supposed to give and receive in an equilibrium manner. As I began to invoke the principle of receiving, miraculous experiences started to take place. I not only started receiving abundantly but also effortlessly all my infinite goods.

Grace of Gratitude for my Receiving

For all my receiving, I add another powerful dimension. When I receive something, I receive it with the Grace of Gratitude. When receiving a payment less than I expected, I do not say that it is too little!

Instead, I accept the payment with love, joy and gratitude and say silently to myself that more is on the way. Perhaps it will come in the form of money and perhaps in the form of a gift, or an opportunity, or knowledge or something else I need.

Grace of Gratitude is a powerful magnet. When we accept everything with gratitude, we are signaling our Divine Universe that we are happy with what we receive and that we desire for more. Our Divine Universe will be glad to hand over more, as per our request.

I do not envision receiving from the same source or one source. I keep myself open to multiple channels of receiving and don't put limits on my ability to receive. You may be surprised and delighted at the myriad of ways our Divine Universe gives to us!

The more we open ourselves to receiving in many unexpected and wonderful ways, the more we receive and then we will have even more to give.

You Are a Special Child of This Divine Universe

I repeat! *You are a special child of this Divine Universe. Riches are your divine birthright!*

41

It is the desire of your loving God that you should receive all the things that you desire. Don't refuse anything, whether it is a compliment, praise, recognition, material goods, help or money. Graciously accept them all with a loving heart and keep the circulation going. Opening your arms to receive also means that you are giving respect, honor, and gratitude to your loving God.

Whatever you are receiving ultimately does not come from people, but from your Divine God! People are only the channel. Refusing to receive is not being kind; it is actually disrespecting a gift from our Divine God.

Also by receiving, you are doing our Divine Universe great good. You are increasing the free flow of riches of our Divine Universe.

So! Stop saying, *"No, thank you."*

✫ Instead with a smile affirm:

> *"Thank you and I want more. I lovingly open my arms to receive compliments, ideas, praises, gifts, money, growth, wisdom and all the infinite riches of my Divine Universe."*

CHAPTER 8

Rise to Riches With The Higher Consciousness

"Whatever it is that you want to be, do, or have, gratitude is the way to receive it. The magical power of gratitude turns your life into gold!"

Rhonda Byrne—*The Magic*

There are three aspects of higher consciousness that open the doors to riches. All divine spiritual texts speak of these higher consciousnesses. Simply, they are *"Blessings, Praises, and Gratitude."*

All of us are already aware of their positive energy, but some of us seem to overlook them because we are so caught up in the hustle and bustle of our life's journey that we forget the graces of blessings, praises and gratitude.

Every creation in our Divine Universe responds to blessings, praises, and gratitude because of their high vibration. It has been scientifically proven that if you bless, praise, and thank the trees and plants, they thrive and grow. Even animals respond the same. Water tastes sweeter when it is praised, blessed, and thanked! Human beings feel empowered when they receive praise from others.

In the same light, I would like to share with you a classic wisdom of the legendary Unity Minister, Catherine Ponder, who wrote in her book *The Dynamic Laws of Prosperity*:

> *"Bless all that you have. Blessing your money stamps it with increase. A dollar which has been blessed is capable of bringing you much greater good than the dollar which has not been blessed. When the word blessing is placed upon tangible objects, these objects are surrounded with the immediate power of increase: 'I bless all that I have and I look with wonder at its increase now.'"*

Praises, gratitude, and blessings acknowledge our abilities to magnetize more riches. They are reminders to trust the unlimited and unending flow of riches of our most generous Divine God. Praise and thank your divine God for providing abundance to you, and everyone including your employer, your competitors, creditors, debtors, suppliers, friends, neighbors, relatives, and everyone in every household.

My Blessing Rituals

I have personally received amazing miracles with the practice of blessings, praises and gratitude.

I have effortlessly received financial abundance from everywhere. I have received things without having to pay for them. I have bounced back quickly from challenges. In fact, most of the wisdom in this book was not dictated by me, but came from our loving divine God. Words and wisdoms flowed to me effortlessly.

Herewith I lovingly share with you my journey to higher consciousness, which begins with my daily routine. I begin each day with a silent prayer of praises, gratitude and blessings.

Upon waking, I greet my morning with gratitude and bless my day, the morning, afternoon, evening, night and its darkness. I bless the sun, moon and stars, sky and the clouds above us.

I lovingly bless and thank our Divine Universe for all her abundance of gifts. I bless all the beauty of our Divine Universe. I lovingly bless the food that nourishes everyone, bless the weather, rain, and thank the water for cleansing and healing us.

I silently bless and thank everything I touch, hear, smell, taste, see and eat. I bless everything I receive, and give. I bless my loved ones and friends, as it is a gift to have them. I bless all people, souls and Angels with divine love, light, peace, joy and happiness.

I bless all countries of this world, all planets and our Divine Universe.

Never scoff at these divine rituals. It has unfolded miracles for me and those who have adopted it. These divine rituals have raised my vibration and I have received even more blessings from uncharted territories.

If I want to change a disturbing, hostile situation into a peaceful one, I radiate divine light and bless the situation and the people involved.

If I am tempted to blame, retaliate or criticize in anger, I decree this powerful blessing; "I bless this situation and the people (name the people involved) with divine wisdom, love, peace, light, understanding, joy and happiness. There is divine good in this situation and good is being released right now."

Do not take anyone's word for it, but try blessing a hostile situation and you will realize its tremendous power.

The Ultimate Master Key to Infinite Riches

If any or some of your desires and dreams are not yet being manifested, do not despair! Make an inventory of what you have right now. Be grateful for all these blessings: your loving family, friends, home, everything in your home and your work place or business.

Be grateful for all of your experiences, and the failures that have given you lessons.

Look for the good in all and the good will inevitably move towards you. When you radiate your gratitude, you immediately not only raise your vibration, but you will simultaneously experience a state of higher consciousness and the universal laws of creation will joyfully open a multitude of doors to more riches for you.

✮ With a smile, affirm the following mantra in your daily life, as it has the quickening power to rise to riches. Don't just read the mantra, but read with total belief and faith:

"I am a powerful magnet and the divine heir to the unlimited riches of this Divine Universe. I bless all the infinite riches that flow to me and that flow out from me. My home is being filled with the unlimited riches of this Divine Universe.

May I live my life in perpetual gratitude and fullness of praise and blessings of divine light and divine love for all. May I not forget my most wonderful life and the most wonderful blessings I have received in the past, and the blessings I am receiving every moment from my Almighty God.

Lovingly, with deepest gratitude, I give thanks to my most loving Lord, God, my Divine Universe, my Guardian Angels, and every soul and everything in this Divine Universe for their nobility and kindness in joy, beauty, light and wisdom."

CHAPTER 9

Multiply Your Riches with the Spiritual Law—Dasvandh

"I honor the Lord with my substance and with a tenth of all my increase. My own barns are now being filled with plenty."

King Solomon

What is *Dasvandh*? *Das* means ten and *vandh* means share. In other words, Dasvandh is *the 'Law of One-Tenth'.*

Dasvandh is a practice among the Sikh religion. This spiritual practice has tremendous, miraculous capacity to dramatically increase your riches. The difference between dasvandh and any other type of giving is that this giving is done systematically and the recommended amount is one-tenth.

This divine principle is a covenant in all spiritual teachings. In Islamic religion, it is called Zakat; in Sikhism, *Dasvandh*; and in Christianity, Tithe. It is integral to the manifestation of increasing your wealth and many swear by this spiritual principle.

It has been said that this spiritual principle has been practiced since the times of ancient Babylonians, Romans, Arabians, Egyptians and Persians (Christopher Hill, *Economics of the Early Church*).

Dasvandh, or the 'Law of One-Tenth', is an acknowledgement of a higher power and unlimited abundance. It eliminates thinking of scarcity and serves the highest good. As you give systematically, you receive systematically many times over.

This spiritual 'Law of One-Tenth' says that we should set aside ten percent of our income to be spread and shared with others that contribute to worthy causes.

This ten percent goes around the world circulating the good and comes back to the giver greatly multiplied.

Miracles of Dasvandh

Dasvandh demonstrates that riches of our Divine Universe are available to everyone in abundance. *Dasvandh* helps us overcome scarcity consciousness and tap into the unlimited abundance of our Divine Universe. It demonstrates that we are part of humanity and are fulfilling our purpose in sharing and helping others.

It also teaches that we must trust God's ability and willingness to provide and also not worry about our own human ability to share our good with others.

Dasvandh is a spiritual law. When we invoke this spiritual law, our spiritual lives are deepened. As we share freely and willingly our money, time and talent, opportunities that benefit us unveil to us everywhere.

The Right Place to Dasvandh

There has been a lot of debate where one should *Dasvandh*. I personally feel *Dasvandh* should be your own private affair. Let your own conscience guide you. My motto of life is *'Love All'*. See divinity in all, as all are God's divine children. With this in mind I spread the *Dasvandh* from all my books throughout the world that include children and animal organizations, and many others.

Some people dasvandh in the form of volunteering their time and services, supporting worthy causes such as spending time with the elderly or orphans, teaching skills to the unfortunate, the handicapped, those with special needs, and many other worthy causes that uplift humanity as a whole.

In its true essence, *Dasvandh is giving back with generosity and gratitude to all.*

One of My Experiences with Dasvandh

While I was in the midst of writing this book, I was in desperate need to find a tenant for my office unit that had been vacant for nearly six months. I found it strange that I was unable to attract any tenant despite its upgraded condition; it had been creatively decorated, painted and newly carpeted.

I sat and thought, "What is wrong? Why am I not getting a tenant?" Then it occurred to me! I had overlooked to *Dasvandh* from the rental profit of my previous tenant who had moved out! I told myself, "When I get a new tenant, I shall dasvandh ten percent from the tenancy deposit."

Within a few days, my real estate agent called and told me she had a potential client who wanted to view my office unit. Upon viewing the unit, this potential tenant signed the lease. I then realized that the power of my intention to *Dasvandh* from the tenancy deposit had brought me a tenant immediately.

Well, that was just thought and intention; can you imagine what result it would bring after I had *Dasvandh* the ten percent from the tenancy deposit?

Invoking this divine principle has brought me wonderful business opportunities, effortless wealth, financial riches, great relationships and more!

Give it a test run for a few months. You will be astounded at the immediate results! But please Dasvandh should be done sincerely from the heart with no reservations or never out of a sense of obligation, because it feels right and it feels good.

With a smile, affirm this wisdom, so eloquently expressed here by famous Indian Poet Rabindranath Tagore:

"This frail vessel thou emptiest again and again, and fillest it ever with fresh life. This little flute of a reed thou hast carried over hills and dales, and hast breathed through it melodies eternally new . . . Thy infinite gifts come to me only on those small hands of mine. Ages pass, and still thou pourest, And still there is room to fill."

CHAPTER **10**

Your Master Plan to Wealth is Manifestation in Action

"Sit down at a certain time everyday and write down on paper what your ideas of God are. You will find that such a practice will pin your mind down to the truth and you will demonstrate results."

Emma Curtis Hopkins
Unveiling Your Hidden Power

Let's examine the successes that people have achieved throughout history; awesome buildings, works of art, innovative products, medical breakthroughs, victories in sports, engineering and technology triumphs and colossal fortunes.

These accomplishments are evidence of visions, dreams and ideas being realized through the use of a Master Plan.

Even though the first principle of getting rich starts in the mental plane, it is not good enough. Its success requires a written Master Plan.

A well-written Master Plan creates awareness, gives a clear vision, and helps you make better decisions and better choices. And your desire to achieve becomes stronger and the enthusiasm will build the acquired momentum.

Master Plan of Action And Total Commitment

Your desires in a master plan will remain only desires without action and total commitment. What we have today around us, the things that make our lives easier and have shaped our lives, are the ideas and goals that were acted upon with total commitment.

Motivational speaker and author of *Unlimited Power,* Anthony Robbins, proclaimed that, *"Action is what unites every great success. Action is what produces results."* What a profound statement!

Even though we all know that action produces results, some people have wonderful goals, plans and aims that are never achieved because they do not act on their inspirations with passion and total commitment. The greatest enemy of success is procrastination. It is the thief of progress, growth, excellence and achievement.

I have a friend who developed an innovative program in the field of children's education. This program has not reached fruition and has sat collecting dust for years. When I realized this program will benefit many children and at the same time bring riches to this friend, I advised her to launch, but she continued giving excuses after excuses. It has been years now and the program is still collecting dust.

This reminds me of a line by my favorite author of *The Greatness Guide,* Robin Sharma, who wisely said, *"Successful people don't make excuses. No great life was ever built on a foundation of excuses. So, stop making them; most of them are self-created delusion, designed to help you avoid doing the things you are afraid to do."*

Without action, our goals, ideas and desires in a master plan are meaningless!

Naturally, there will be many challenges on your way to achieving your goals, but that should never ever hold you back. *Your dream is worth it!*

Once you've begun, there is no turning back and you've got to endure all obstacles. Of course you can quit, but how would you feel if you give up? How would you feel if your dream was unfulfilled?

The business organization that employs you was not built out of thin air. Your bosses had the spirit of entrepreneurship and they acted on their goals with total commitment. Their action with commitment created employment opportunities for a lot of people.

Scores of wealthy achievers experienced failures, but they never lost focus and momentum. Their capacity for action was based on a commitment to a continuous attempt until they got it right. This capacity for action has resulted in numerous wonderful inventions.

These people have left a golden footprint in the world with their overwhelming passion for their goals. Their achievement could not have reached the pinnacle of success without action and total commitment. In spite of all the challenges they faced, there was no turning back. They believed action with total commitment preceded success. Such great minds deserve a *"round of applause"* for realizing their goals.

You too can have Riches with a Master Plan of Action and Total Commitment

Start by listing all the strategies you can think of. Predicting possible challenges will give you the ability to create sound strategies. Get support from others who have walked the path and achieved similar goals. A lot of successful people will be glad to share their experiences and strategies used in achieving their goals.

The need for contingency planning is critical to your ability to respond to challenges that may unfold. Actualize your goals constantly by being flexible, refine and redesign your strategies by being aware of the current environment and your predictions of the future.

As you go about creating your Master Plan, add other important dimensions to it by asking yourself the following questions:

⭑ *Are my desires, goals, visions, ideas and dreams in the Master Plan for the higher good? Are they ethical, and would they hurt anyone else if they come to pass?*
⭑ *Would my desires, goals, visions, ideas and dreams in the Master Plan improve the quality of my life, the lives of others, and my country?*
⭑ *Am I willing to commit to them and what am I willing to sacrifice to pursue them?*

Imagine that the results are fulfilled.

In the final step of developing a complete Master Plan with action and total commitment for the fulfillment of your desires, there is one additional and important component: *Imagine that the results are fulfilled.* Many wealthy achievers and prosperity seers swear by this magical step.

When you pen your desires, goals, visions and dreams in a Master Plan and take action with total commitment and imagine its fulfillment, you invoke the powers of the Divine Universe and it will start bringing in the right opportunities, people and resources to help you materialize your goal into reality spontaneously.

✫ With a smile, joyfully say to yourself:

> *"I radiate divine light to my goals, visions and desires in my Master Plan. I now take action with total commitment and imagine its fulfillment.*
>
> *My Divine Universe is already bringing the right opportunities, people and resources to help me realize my desires."*

CHAPTER 11

Riches in the Learning Age

"I adore the whole notion of growth.
I believe that's why we are here."

Robin Sharma
Be Extraordinary: The Greatness Guide Book Two

A futurist writer well-known for corporate revolution, Alvin Toffler, in his book *The Third Wave*, described the present era as an information revolution and that this wave will last forever. *"The illiterate of the 21st century will not be those who cannot read and write, but those who cannot learn, unlearn and relearn."* How true!

Toffler summed up the explosion of the *'Information and Knowledge'* economy simply as the *'Learning and Relearning Age.'*

How do businesses stay competitive and successful in the ever-increasing pace of changing technology?

The answer is learning and relearning.

A business corporation's major asset is its people, particularly the ones whose professional repertoires are constantly expanding through learning and relearning. People who remain stuck doing things the same way fall through the cracks; people who are willing to learn and relearn quickly surpass them.

The learners consistently move forward because of their scope of knowledge, willingness to update themselves with the latest knowledge, and most importantly, because of their ability to apply that knowledge.

Sanaya Roman in her book *Spiritual Growth* gave an impressive piece of wisdom, *"Your higher self is always growing, exploring, learning, and discovering new aspects of itself. Growing—reaching new levels of understanding, self-awareness, and aliveness—is one of the main goals of all life. Growth never ends, for even when you reach higher levels there are still further levels to go. Without growth there is a contraction of life-force energy. With growth you feel vibrant, alive, healthy and joyful."*

Learning and creating are both divine forms of growth. There is always something new to learn. Thinking you have mastered something completely is an illusion leading to stagnation.

Learning to Create Excellence

An important aspect of business success is value. Learning and value go hand-in-hand. The more skills and knowledge you acquire, the better the quality of your output will be. But having skills and knowledge doesn't create value unless you apply them with a commitment to excellence.

Excellence comes from a total dedication to world-class products and services, and a quest for superior value. Superior value comes from giving your best using all of your skills, knowledge and creative energy in every area of your life!

When you think about it, the products or services you provide are an expression and extension of who you are; whether you're an employee or an employer, the way you share them with the world is a true reflection of you.

For example, you may be making or selling something you consider to be boring or trivial, but there are people who want that product or service! If you care about making these people happy, it will show in your attitude and the quality of your work. That way, even the most mundane task takes on a beauty of its own.

The end result is that you're happy because you make others happy. Wealth unfolds from a genuine desire to enrich the lives of others.

A salesperson who genuinely cares about taking care of a customer's needs, a teacher who genuinely cares about enriching students' lives and a mechanic who genuinely wants to make every customer's car work perfectly are assets to society.

In every career, occupation or whatever your endeavor is, strive for personal excellence to enrich the lives of others by delivering value. When you deliver value, you feel good about yourself.

Giving less than your best leads to feeling less-than-good, with a burden of guilt that you could have done better. This is highly negative energy that repels riches! Release all of that negativity by making a commitment to provide the best value that enriches the lives of others.

Offering value means honoring the divine gifts, which each of us have been given: talents, the ability to learn and the ability to create. Always remember that the world needs your unique talents and contributions. *Using these marvelous gifts in the spirit of providing the best value to your society will lead you to super riches.*

Embrace Lifelong Learning

As the Zen masters say, keep a *"beginner's mind"* and keep expanding your knowledge with curiosity and delight. The more you learn, the more you expand your horizons. The broader your horizons, the more opportunities you will have. Whether you are an employer or an employee, the way to super riches is learning and relearning.

Take advantage of your ability to learn. Let the world of possibilities open up to you!

Be a liberal learner of the world. With vast knowledge, you seize many opportunities. Do not get trapped in the world of complacency and ignorance; otherwise, you will get left behind. *Knowledge is power.*

Upgrade the quality of your thinking by developing an intellectual, productive, creative and inquisitive mind, which will enable you to adapt to the continually changing environment.

This life's journey is a school. You are here to learn, improve, and grow. Every learning opportunity we get contributes to the well-being of our society. Learning develops mental faculties, sharpens skills and creates self-improvement in this ever-changing world.

Furthermore, it opens opportunities for lucrative employment, creates a sense of independence, builds self-confidence, boosts your competitiveness in the global marketplace and contributes to the sustainable economic growth of your country. *Most beneficial of all, it takes you to the league of wealth!*

It also enhances character excellence. This leads to a more evolved society intellectually, emotionally and spiritually. It also adds immeasurable goodness to our Divine Universe.

☆ With a promise, say to yourself:

> *"I will keep learning what I don't know. I will approach learning with the boundless enthusiasm of a child who is eager to learn about everything. I will embrace lifelong learning as an enjoyable quest.*
>
> *I radiate divine light to all my learning and the learning of everyone and radiate divine light to all my invisible and visible teachers."*

CHAPTER **12**

Riches in Ebb

"Every person has cycles in life, times when money is coming in more than it is going out and times when it is going out more than it is coming in."

Sanaya Roman
Creating Money

If you study the various cycles of ebb periods in this world such as inflation, recession and stimulus, you will see that such ebb periods are actually temporary.

Therefore, there is nothing to panic about!

In the consciousness of our Divine Universe, an ebb period is simply a temporary adjustment and readjustment to harmonize and balance the economic conditions of the world.

Are you currently in an ebb period?

For instance, let's say you have been laid off or your business sales are low and it seems money is stagnant. An ebb period is the time to hold fast to your self-confidence. *Know that this is a temporary phase and that the flow will come back to you in due time.*

You may have an initial period of panic as most people do, but the sooner you can begin to use the situation for your benefit, the sooner you'll regain your confidence and things will turn around for you.

An ebb period can be stressful for most people. However, once you are aware that ebb is a temporary period, you don't have to carry the burden of stress.

Here is some powerful wisdom for managing stress-related ebbs in the flow of money. These tips give you clarity of mind and help you from falling prey to the 'victim mentality' that makes you blame the world for your dilemma. The resulting positive attitude will turn the tides and create a positive flow period.

Get Creative during an Ebb Period

Perhaps you have heard that *"necessity is the mother of invention."*

An ebb period is the perfect time to get creative and challenge you to explore new things. Open your mind to new ways. It is probably the path you are supposed to follow, as long as it leads to good actions and does not harm others or interrupt your positive flow.

If you are in an ebb period, say to yourself, *"This ebb is temporary, and this is the time for me to create the flow."*

Then become creative. Access your intuitive guidance for novel and unexpected ways to put your talents to use to create the positive flow.

The ebb period is there to get you to open new doors. Start doing the things you've always wanted to do, but have been putting off, especially if they are close to your heart. If you've had an urge to begin doing something you've always secretly wanted to do, this is the perfect time to set those wheels in motion!

Explore alternative ways to increase your flow of financial abundance. Be hyper-alert to opportunities.

Ask yourself how this ebb period can be beneficial to your ultimate goal of being rich. Ask yourself what you can learn from this period. You may be learning new lessons, such as how to *"get down to the basics"* of what is important in life or being more compassionate and generous to others who are worse off than you.

Take the time to think about these things as you go through your ebb cycle. Trust that this experience will teach you and prepare you for the next cycle of prosperity in your life. Let go of your old ways. Trust your intuitive guidance and take some time off to work on your life's purpose.

See the opportunities, not the roadblocks. Relax and shift your focus and consciously start telling a positive story of your life. As you do this, your vibration will shift to feeling good and this vibration will signal the Divine Universe to open the doors to your super riches.

Trusting In Our Generous Divine Universe

Have trust in our generous Divine Universe. Do not, I repeat, do not feel like a failure even if you're experiencing the worst ebb in money. No financial crisis should have the power to make you question your self-worth. *You are more resourceful than you realize.*

Your experiences, knowledge, skills, education, creative power and passion are tools at your disposal that are potentially great sources of building your riches. Just because these things have not been converted into income yet, do not discount them.

If you put your trust in the Divine Universe and follow your heart with passion and dedication, your various resources will create abundant wealth for you.

But please, do not allow yourself to get overpowered by negative influences. Close all doors to thoughts and talks that make you feel unhappy or inferior.

Remember, nothing comes to you without your invitation. Never seek the advice or opinion of anyone who will vibrate negative reactions, as you cannot afford to allow the negative vibes into your consciousness.

This road to wealth is an extremely important journey.

Don't let anyone ruin it!

Equally important, have an attitude of gratitude for the abundance you have right now and the abundance that is coming to you. Do not whine about your ebb situation. Instead, think and talk as if you have abundance.

Trusting in the Divine Universe means aligning your vibrational frequency with the consciousness of our Divine Universe. Then the Divine Universe will unveil to you new horizons and new opportunities to manifest your super riches.

Any kind of desire for success, including financial success, not only requires effort and action, but also requires the alignment of your thoughts with your desire. Remember, offering negative thoughts or thoughts contrary to what you desire causes resistance to the manifestation of your wealth.

Challenge yourself to picture your life as an upward spiral. You will see that you pass through certain stages over and over again—that is the ebb and flow. The hope is that you will see similar situations in each ebb or flow with a wisdom that comes from experience. Each time your view should be from a different, higher perspective.

Then you will look down and see how far you have come. You will see the other ebbs and flows that have occurred in your life and know that this situation is not a permanent thing.

If you remember that ebbs are not permanent and if you are wealthy mentally and inside, your outside will soon come to reflect that vision; not the other way around. If your circumstances are bleak, they do not have the power to change the abundance in your mind unless you allow it.

Make a pact with yourself to mentally live in abundance, no matter what is going on in the physical world. Your thoughts will turn things around soon enough. Paint images in your mind of the things you want, not those you don't want.

Always live in the consciousness of riches, understanding that your generous Divine Universe is lovingly overflowing with all the abundance you could ever desire.

⭐ With a smile, decree this powerful mantra:

"There are many wonderful opportunities available around me. All these opportunities are coming to me effortlessly.

I love having money from all the countries. I bless all the money I have right now. I bless all the money of all countries. Money from everywhere is flowing to me right now. I give thanks to my loving God and Angels for all their kindness."

CHAPTER 13

Attracting Riches With Your Life Force Energy

"One highly vibrational soul can counterbalance masses that have low vibrational frequency."
Dr. David Hawkins
Power Vs Force

Our Divine Universe and everything in it is a manifestation of life force energy. In Sanskrit it is called *Prana*. The Chinese call this energy *Chi*. It is one of the main treasures in attracting prosperity. This life force energy is the least understood component of wealth and one that is most taken for granted. When all is well with us, we feel that vibrant flow. It is the flow of abundance of wealth, health, joy and happiness.

However, without this energy everything is blocked. One single blockage anywhere along the line is enough to block energy in other areas of your life!

Sanaya Roman, says in her book *Creating Money*, *"If money isn't flowing in your life, look at where your own energy might not be moving. You want both money and your personal energy to flow. By unblocking your energy, you can create more money in your life. Blocks in money can be caused by places where your energy isn't flowing, such as in your physical body, your emotions, or your relationship with others."*

In the 'Law of Manifestation' there is a direct correlation between your personal energy and the flow of riches. If you find little or no movement in the flow of your financial riches, that means your energy is seriously blocked. To unblock that energy, we must first examine a significant cause of the block.

Your Emotions and Your Life Force Energy

Scores of studies have revealed that our emotional state can positively or negatively alter our life force energy by the chemical messages it sends. If you are happy, your body shows it. If you are unhappy, that shows, too.

Harboring negative feelings such as anger, depression, jealousy, bitterness, frustration, guilt, resentment, worry, stress, anxiety, or any other negative emotion are blockages to positive life force energy.

New Thought Spiritual Leader Dr. Emmet Fox teaches us from his *The Sermon on the Mount* that explains it beautifully:

> *"If your prayers are not being answered, find out if there is not some old thing about which you are resentful. Search and see if you are not really holding*

a grudge against some individual, or nation, race, social class, some religious movement or political party of which you disapprove. If you do, then you have an act of forgiveness to perform." (The Sermon on the Mount—page 173, Emmet Fox).

So! Unload these negativities and get all your prayers answered.

On a sheet of paper, write the heading *"Acts of Forgiveness."* Write the names of people whom you wish to forgive. Next to their names write all the negativity you feel toward them, such as past resentments, hurt, anger and frustrations. Then write the following prayer:

"I transmute all my negative thoughts, negative memories and unwanted energies into pure love and divine light.

I forgive them. I make peace with everyone. I forgive myself. My past was a learning experience and it was good. I now enter into the sacrament of the new. The new is flooding me with blessings of love, money, friendship, beauty and health. I deserve this new happiness! I bless and thank my loving God for all my happiness.

I clear all channels within me. I now feel liberated and I am in bliss. In this state of bliss, I now regain my life force energy. I now experience a sense of power, and the miraculous wealth of the infinite is flowing my way right now."

Increase your Life Force Energy with Order and Harmony

Order—Your living sanctuary and your workplace are your sacred temples. You may need to uplift their energy as often as needed. They may be crying out for help. Check if there is a system of proper order. See if it is cluttered with unfinished or unattended tasks, unsorted files, or piles of undone work.

A cluttered working and living environment carries depressing negative imprints, leading to a negative life force energy that affects the flow of that abundance you desire so much.

The divine metaphysical law says that if you want to keep the river of good flowing into your life, you must create a vacuum to receive it. Sweep clean all the negative debris by putting everything in order.

Remove signs, words, or pictures that depict sadness or poverty. Beautify your environment by giving it a new look. Change the color of your walls and rearrange your furniture.

Decorate with symbols of love, success, financial riches, and symbols that have expressions of joy and happiness. As you go about putting everything in order, say, "*I joyfully release the unwanted to welcome the new.*"

A total overhaul will uplift the vibration of your surroundings and clear blockages and you will experience lightness and amplify good feelings of being in an atmosphere of renewed serenity; you have created a new void into which new abundance will flow to you.

Harmony—You may ask what harmony has to do with rising to riches.

Absolutely everything! There is great power in harmony. It is the consciousness of our Divine Universe.

Harmony comes from within; it is an inner glow that radiates joy and peace and increases your life force energy for the attainment of riches. Disharmony distracts, repels and dissipates one's good.

Make a checklist of the people around you and evaluate if they are discouraging, negative complainers and blamers about their life. Check if they are always fighting or having misunderstandings. Such energy depletes your life force energy. Immediately remove yourself from such places.

Carve out regular, quiet moments for yourself. Immerse yourself in Mother Nature and its beauties. Silently radiate your divine love to all God's beautiful creations: rivers, oceans, mountains, the sun, the moon, the stars, clouds, sky, and rainbow.

And also radiate divine light and love to all the kingdoms of God: the animal kingdom, the mineral kingdom, plant kingdom, kingdom of the Angels and all the other kingdoms of God. And extend your loving gratitude to your Guardian Angels for their kindness. Even though they are not visible to you, they are there watching over you lovingly.

☆ With a smile, decree this powerful uplifting mantra:

"May everyone be happy, loving, beautiful, prosperous, peaceful and in perfect health.

May I call upon the most powerful divine healing light and radiate this divine healing light to everyone to heal and increase their life force energy."

CHAPTER **14**

Your Present Shapes Your Future

*"When we are seeking money, or a good relationship
or a great job, what we are really seeking is happiness.
The mistake we make is not going for happiness first. If
we did, everything else would follow."*
Deepak Chopra, Creating Affluence

What shapes your future?

The quality of your present state!

All major religions and spiritual leaders have taught that if we accept the present moment as a gift, we experience joy, happiness and peace. Even though the gift of the present moment is central to all spiritual teachings of the world, we often ignore it.

Some people are so busy whining about past dramas or about the way things "should have been in the past" or the way things "should be, but probably won't be in the future," that they forget to live and appreciate life in the present.

Have you heard yourself say these statements out loud or even in thoughts?

- ☆ *I will be happy only when I land the perfect job.*
- ☆ *I will be happy only when I have the perfect soul mate.*
- ☆ *I will be happy only when I have an X amount of money.*
- ☆ *I will be happy only when I lose these extra pounds.*
- ☆ *I will be happy only when I take my dream vacation.*
- ☆ *I will be happy only when I am promoted.*
- ☆ *I will be happy only when I am wealthy.*

The above statements of dissatisfaction clearly indicate unhappy, worrying vibrations. The irony is that these dissatisfied statements not only rob the quality of your present moment, but the negative vibrations are transmitted to the Divine Universe and bring forth more frustrations, obstacles and negativity to your desires, dreams and goals.

Spiritual Seer Sri Ramana Maharishi also declared that, *"There is no happiness in any object of the world. The self is pure happiness, which we mistake as coming from outside."* Well said!

Being Joyful and Happy in the Present Moment

Joy and happiness are blessings and are contagious, and they raise the vibration level of everyone around you. Become that fountain of joy, that cheerful person everyone flocks to. Become the one who is courageous and hopeful and you will inspire others to be the same.

The more we talk of happiness in the present moment, the more we create light and joy in the world and the more happiness comes into our lives. Abundance and harmony surround those who are happy and joyful in the present.

If you approach life with a doom-and-gloom attitude, your life energy gets depleted, and when you experience low energy, you are not in sync with the consciousness of our Divine Universe. If you fill your world with cheer, you grow spiritually.

When you accept the present moment knowing that you already possess everything you could ever want, you will eventually see that it was only your ego that thought it didn't have it all!

Your life is a worthwhile journey only if you cruise with joy and happiness every moment. Make joyfulness and happiness your first priority no matter what your present circumstances are. Think, speak, eat, drink, rest and sleep joyfully. Know that in this moment there is peace, joy, harmony and unlimited abundance.

See the world around you with wonder and curiosity, like a little child. Savor the sensual experiences of each moment—the sight, the sound, the texture, the smell and the taste. Always approach life with a joyous and sunny attitude!

Sometimes out of the blue, unpleasant things from the past pop into our mind and get us into an awful mood. Knowing that it's easy to get sucked into that negativity and relive past events, consciously redirect your thoughts and give yourself the appreciation for what you are right now and what you have.

Tell yourself *"the past was a learning experience and has elevated me to a higher spiritual level."* Such wise thoughts give you the gift of joy and happiness in the present moment.

Give *"Thanks to God"* for your present prosperity. Even if some of your heart's desires are not yet manifested, you still have so much to be thankful for!

Your perfect health, your home, your smile, your laughter, your family, the shoes on your feet, the clothes you wear, your job, your family, your friends, the delicious food you eat every day, the love you receive, the sunshine from the sun, the beauty of nature—yes, your life is full of abundance.

In his book *The Power of Now*, Author Eckhart Tolle gave the following useful statements, *"When you honor, acknowledge, and fully accept your present reality—where you are, who you are and what you are, then you will be grateful for what you have, grateful for what is and grateful for being. Gratitude for the present moment and the fullness of life now is true prosperity. It cannot come in the future. In time, that prosperity manifest for you in various ways."*

Absolutely true!

Make a decision right now to value, acknowledge and cherish your present moment as a "Gift." This becomes the catalyst to begin manifesting what you want. Your present thoughts and feelings create the state of your future. Your emotional feelings have powerful magnetic frequency.

If you are always thinking of something hurtful and you worry anxiously about your future, or if you are thinking of your problems and are feeling guilty or angry, you will attract the same!

Ask yourself, "What can I do to change my present situation?"

⭐ Then, joyfully decree:

"I focus on the present moment, as it is a Gift. My natural state is abundance of happiness and vitality. No matter where I am or what I am doing, nothing is more important than being happy. I am happy, grateful and at peace. I look for all situations to be happy. My happiness is in my present moment.

My past was a learning experience. I only remember the good and happy past. I am happy in my present reality and I now focus on my blessings of the present. I have nothing to worry about the future, as my future is beautiful and I send divine light and divine love to my future."

CHAPTER 15

The Ultimate Wealth Increasing Principle

"Saving money is a discipline and any discipline affects all other disciplines in your life."
Brian Tracy, Self Help Author

If you want to know whether you are destined to achieve stupendous financial riches, ask this question:

"Am I able to save money?"

This statement is no mere inventive theory. If you research the key success factors of wealthy people, you will discover that they cultivate the habit of saving money and they will not entrust their finances to someone who does not have a clue about the power of savings.

Take a look at your financial situation. Do you have nightmares about your financial status?

Have you been earning for many years, but whine, "I have no more money left?"

Have you realized how all your money slipped away?

If you have not been saving, then you truly need to harness the divine power of financial savings.

Saving is a powerful magnet that attracts continuous financial riches.

Some people tend to believe that when we save money, we are implying that we don't have enough. Nothing could be further from the truth!

Have you ever seen a squirrel stash nuts for winter? Do you think the squirrel feels lack right now? No!

A hungry squirrel experiencing lack would eat those nuts immediately, not store them away. It is clear the squirrel has enough to eat. The stashed-away nuts are savings. He is saving some for later when he knows he will need them. The squirrel knows there will be ebbs and flow.

It's the same with money. Think of your savings as expanding your options and possibilities. Think of what you could do with the money you have diligently saved, rather than unwisely spent. When money is dissipated with unwise spending, it destroys the 'good feelings' of abundance. When good feelings of abundance are destroyed, thoughts of lack of abundance are drawn in our mindset.

Success of an Enterprise With Wealth Increasing Principle

I would like to share a striking example of my own personal experience on the power of savings. Some years ago, a few of my friends influenced me to invest in a new business. Within two years, the business started to make good profits. As the business grew, there was a lot of inflow and outflow of funds, but no funds were kept aside as reserves for contingency or emergency and expansion.

During one of our board meetings, I propose a wealth increasing principle: *"Savings"*. I would stress the importance of reserve funds for the company and stress that every month some funds should be withdrawn from the receivables to be placed in a bank deposit. The withdrawn funds should be treated as mandatory expense payable to bank deposit.

The CEO of the company shut me off by insisting that we should be focusing on business development and not on saving. I then realized that this CEO was short-sighted.

However, since I had a stake in the company I never gave up my nagging on savings until the CEO had to give in. Hence, every month the accountant had to withdraw the proposed sum by the board to be deposited as reserve funds into the bank deposit.

After about few years, these reserves became useful. Our company bought a lot of properties and further expanded the business with the reserve funds.

Now, you see the power of savings!

Capital reserves are essential to the success of all business organizations. Business leaders who do not have the foresight on the importance of reserve capital can expect their business to struggle.

If you are a business entrepreneur, discipline yourself to withdraw every week or every month more than ten percent of your business income and treat it as an expense payable in the capital reserve account. Invoke this *"wealth increasing principle"* as your company's mandatory policy. You will thank me for this wisdom in the years to come.

It's important to feel abundant and wealthy even if your savings account is small by most standards. Money saved makes you feel happy, secure, and wealthy. These feelings attract more financial wealth. It is that powerful.

Saving Versus Spending

Since savings are a powerful magnet for more riches, spending money is equally powerful because money needs to be circulated. Without circulation, our economy halts. Therefore, forming the habit of saving money does not mean that you should not spend your money. It is important to spend money as well.

The point here is how you spend money. For example, spending unwisely and neglecting necessities will not bring you riches!

Legendary Unity Minister, Charles Fillmore, in his book, *Prosper*, advises, *"Money is to be used, not abused. It is good to keep one's obligations paid. It is good to have some money on hand for good uses, such as hospitality, education, developing industries that will contribute to the good of a number of people, the furtherance of spiritual work, helping others build useful and constructive lives and many other good purposes and activities."*

If you do not have the discipline to control how you spend the money you earn, then you have no chance to be wealthy. Even if you do become wealthy you may not be capable of holding on to it for long. Spend money wisely by thinking, planning and budgeting ahead. Do not spend your money on harmful drugs, or things that bring ills to human life or any life or that negatively affect our natural resources and environment.

Restore your positive relationship with money and better understand its purpose. It is to be spread around, yes, but some of it is to be saved for later, so it can be spread around at the appropriate time.

If you desire more money or if you would like to become a money magnet, then develop a habit of saving money. As your savings grow, you'll experience that wonderful, warm and confident feeling of being rich.

Can you see how your relationship with money changes positively?

You pay for your obligations, you can save some, and you feel more in control of its flow.

☆   With a smile, make a resolution and say to yourself:

"I will start keeping aside some money, even if it is a small sum. The more I save the more money I will attract into my life.

I radiate divine light to all my money that is being saved and spent. As I save, the more I receive to save and spend for my obligations."

CHAPTER **16**

LOVE—The Divine Power to Riches

"If you aren't manifesting what you want, there probably is an absence of love somewhere in your inner world."

Wayne Dyer
Manifest your Desire

*L*ove is the natural state of our Divine Universe. It is the pure life force and ultimate consciousness of our Divine Universe. Love has the most superior power to manifesting riches. There is nothing that is not blessed with the power of love. Everything in our Divine Universe is created out of love.

Your presence in this Universe is because of love.

The food you eat daily is created out of love. Your education came about because of love. This book you are reading is written out of love for you.

Love is the essence of being; it is the greatest and ultimate superior power to manifesting riches.

Baron Eugene Fersen, founder of The Lightbearers organization and the author of *Science of Being* put it this way, *"Love is the supreme Universal power. Love is Attraction. It is the Governing and Sustaining Power, which holds the entire Universe together in one coherent whole."* Powerful definition!

Love is a divine magnetic force that circulates through every soul. Every person has the capacity to create miracles through love and to use the power of love to manifest abundance of money, wealth, health and more love.

A True Story of Rising To Riches with Love

Once I visited a friend who owned a successful clothing boutique. Her boutique was located in a competitive shopping mall. In spite of all the fierce competition, she was successful compared to the other boutiques. I asked her about her success formula. She told me that her formula was simple.

Regularly, she would affirm this prayer, *"I see divinity in all my customers and I radiate divine light and love to all of them. My clothes bring beauty and comfort to all my customers."*

In addition, the boutique displayed a sign at the entrance, which said, *"We love you and welcome you with our loving hearts."*

At the exit, another sign that said, *"We love our customers, please come again."*

That's her brilliant success formula, which I call, 'Open Sesame to Riches'.

You, too, can have your desire manifested with the power of love.

Love frees our mind and opens our doors to infinite riches. When our thoughts are filled with love, we become a magnet to attract what we love.

My Magnetism to Manifesting Wealth with Love

Friends ask me what is my secret to my wealth, bliss, peace, joy, happiness and perfect health. I tell them that my secret is LOVE!

I see love and divinity in everyone and everything!

In my daily prayer, I silently radiate divine love, light, peace and joy to everyone and everything in all the Kingdoms of God. I radiate divine love and divine light to all the infinite riches of our Divine Universe.

I radiate divine love and divine light to my competitors, customers, clients and everyone; all souls of this Divine Universe, all animals, my family members, my relationships, business partners, suppliers, creditors, debtors and friends, and to the leaders of all countries and nations.

I radiate divine love to all the beauties of this Divine Universe; the sun, moon, stars, sky, water, oceans, and mother earth, plants, trees, rivers, mountains and hills.

I radiate my love to our loving God and all our divine, loving Angels. I radiate divine light and love and bless everything I see, eat, taste, hear and feel.

When any part of my body is in pain, I heal it with radiating divine love and divine light. I say, "I LOVE YOU," to my internal organs, cells, blood and all parts of my body and its divine intelligence. This divine practice has brought me perfect health, high vitality, perfect eyesight and bliss.

When someone or a situation upsets me, I radiate divine love and divine light and bless that person and the situation.

I had a working associate spreading unkind, negative remarks about me to other staff behind my back. To stop the situation I confronted her. She not only denied it, but also started to retaliate with unkind words.

Instead of reacting or retaliating, I deliberately affirm these powerful sentences:

> *"I radiate divine love to this situation and the people involved; I transmute this situation into divine love. With divine love, good will be paramount in this situation."*

The result was that within a few days, she apologized and made peace with me. That's the power of divine love. When you are in a challenging situation, radiate divine love to the situation and the people involved, the wrong or evil against you will dissipate. Divine love changes all conditions and circumstances.

It's easy to think positive thoughts when things are going well, but it may not be easy during challenging times. There is, however, a choice. You can stay in the challenging situation and attract more negativity or set yourself free by radiating divine love.

Love begins within yourself

We cannot love others if we don't love ourselves. Love begins within yourself. When you love yourself, others will naturally love you, too. Stop whining about how bad and how hard your life is. *Fall in love with your life!*

The purpose of your life is to love every moment, wherever you are for the experience, the gifts it has given you, and for its many wise lessons. Love every part of you; love your hair, love your eyes, and love your hands. Love your mistakes and achievements.

Surround yourself with love every moment of your life. Make every thought, every word and every action in the vibration of love. What you think, talk about and feel has a powerful magnetic frequency. When your thoughts, speech and feelings are filled with love, you attract the same.

Radiate love to everything around you, your home, car, food, water, business, money, workplace, colleagues, business associates, family and friends. The more you radiate love, the more magnetic you become to your desired riches.

Be "In Love" with that image of what you want. Feel the happiness of having the thing that you desire. Feel love coursing through you. From a place of love, tell God what you want. Your loving God will deliver what you most love in your heart!

Love in Giving and Receiving

When you open yourself to giving and receiving with love, you are allowing the miracle of love to work through you. Feeling love for the riches you have received and for the riches you are receiving now creates even more ways for these riches to come to you.

Make every exchange an opportunity to radiate love to those around you. The more you give love the more you will attract people, opportunities, money, beneficial situations and more love. When you invoke strong vibrations of love in all your endeavors, it amplifies good feelings and these emotions will signal the Divine Universe that you want more of it.

Then the Divine Universe will lovingly take your command and place it on your lap.

Love What You Do

The book, *The Power of Intention*, brilliantly written by Dr. Wayne Dyer, says, "If you aren't doing what you love and loving what you do, your power of intention is weakened, you attract into your life more of the dissatisfaction." I fully agree with Dr. Dyer!

We whine about our frustrations about our work, career and life in general. These are clear signals that we are not living a purposeful, passionate life. We are unhappy and frustrated because there is a lack of love in what we do.

When we are engaged and passionate about what we love, we radiate joy, we feel alive and our energy level increases and we do everything with excellence, efficiency and fulfillment. When we produce excellence in what we do, it is a gift we give to ourselves and to the world at large. Manifesting riches becomes immediate and astounding.

While writing this book, I not only enjoyed the writing experience, but also had a mystical, special, heavenly feeling of love, bliss, joy, peace and happiness. I realized that I was full of vitality and in a high vibrational frequency. I became magnetic to everything. I was attracting everything I desired effortlessly and spontaneously.

Love in Negative Situations

Love problematic people, love your irritating neighbor, love your demanding spouse, love your fussy in-laws and love your nagging parents. Love the strengths and weaknesses of all humanity. The strengths should be loved with admiration and joy, and the weaknesses should be loved with compassion, empathy and forgiveness. Spread love in times of anger and hatred.

See divinity in everyone and everything, and as you do so, you will be flooded with thoughts of love. Live only in the thought of love for all, and you will draw love to yourself from all.

In every instance where you catch yourself having negative and unkind thoughts about someone, replace those thoughts with thoughts of love. You will be surprised to find yourself becoming more joyful, happier and blissful each moment. With joy and happiness, you will manifest all your heart's desires.

Only love can set you free to realize your heart's desire.

Love frees our mind and opens our doors to the immediate riches of our Divine Universe. When all your endeavors are undertaken with love, you become a powerful magnet, attracting wealth effortlessly and spontaneously.

☆ With a smile, make a resolution right now and say:

> *"I will love every moment of my life. I love the feeling of being born into this beautiful prosperous Divine Universe. I love having abundance of money and wealth, living in a big, beautiful mansion, having my own airplane and having vacations at my favorite places.*
>
> *I love counting money and having lots of money in my wallet. I love having multiple currencies of various countries. I love the joy of sharing my riches with others. The more I love having money and abundance, the more I picture it and draw it to myself."*

CHAPTER **17**

Riches in the Creative Plane

"Men have the idea that material substance is limited, and they engage in competition trying to grab one another's money. The Divine Mind has ideas of substance as unlimited and is equally available to all."
Charles Fillmore
Prosper

*S**ome* people have ignorantly been mentally conditioned to believe that there is a limited supply of resources such as money, food, clothes, oil, water, jobs, businesses and homes etc. Out of panic and fear they steal, hoard, compete, beat others for promotion and manipulate for survival.

Daily in our corporate life, we hear the famous, negative buzz words, "Let's beat the competition." Competition in the corporate business arena originates when there are limited resources available. But this is a false belief. Our Divine Universe is infinitely creative. Anything needed and requested is granted and created!

Everything around us is being manifested out of creativity, which is the consciousness of our Divine Universe. Our Divine Universe creates all our goods out of pure creative energy, and since this creative energy is limitless, there can be no lack and no limit to creation and no need to compete for resources.

Being in a capitalistic society, it is difficult to avoid competition. However, when there is positive competition, it should be encouraged if it benefits consumers and encourages excellence in innovation for businesses.

Role Models To Emulate in the Creative Plane

All throughout history, people who have amassed extraordinary riches have been primarily from the creative plane. They innovated unique and authentic ways of producing, creating, and marketing products and services, as well as, exceptional ways of leveraging finances, creative ways of expansion, ingenious business models, and unorthodox business strategies, organic expansions, unconventional management style, etc.

Noted wealthy people who inspire me deeply are E.M. Statler, Van Heusen, and many more. They strive to make every idea, every product and every service distinct. E.M. Statler accumulated millions of dollars in wealth in the hotel business by rendering home-like services. Van Heusen's creative idea of producing soft collars rewarded him with super wealth.

All these financial magnets and many others have placed themselves at the top of the pantheon and have made history by aligning their mindset with the creative plane. There is no scarcity in their minds; only creative abundance. They reaffirm that creative thinking is the raw material of innovation and their companies innovate to succeed in the changeable global marketplace.

It is increasingly clear that business organizations need to produce new, high quality products and services as the world continues to integrate. Without any doubt, creative innovation and value is the lifeblood of every stellar organization.

If you want to take your business to super riches, embrace creative innovation and commit to a value-driven mindset. You don't have to go far; our society is already evolved in continuous creative innovation. What you have around you today is all from the creative plane.

A True Story of a Creative Entrepreneur

This reminds me of a friend of mine, an entrepreneur who is wealthy because of her creative thinking. She proclaims that everyone is creative and has something of value to offer. She has an open ear for all her staff members, including janitors. She says that if you want better solutions and decisions, you have to loosen up and think outside of the box; otherwise, you will not revolutionize your endeavors.

Within her business organization, she has created a department called the Creative Department, which is headed by a creative manager who reports to her directly. Staff members from other departments are invited to this creative department for brainstorming sessions before any decisions are made or if they want a solution to a problem.

With her permission, I interviewed some of her staff. The feedback I received from the interview was amazing. I found that the morale of her staff was high because their ideas were always honored and appreciated.

In this process, *the cardinal rule in her organization is not to criticize any idea, but to explore all ideas and weigh their usefulness before coming to any judgment or verdict.*

You too can be wealthy like my friend. Get in touch with your creative faculties; you will be amazed with your astounding ingenuity.

There is No Limit To the Universal Creative Ideas

Charles Fillmore in his book *Prosper,* said, "*The spiritual substance from which comes all visible wealth is never depleted. It is right with you all the time and responds to your faith in it and your demands upon it. It is not affected by your ignorant talk of hard times, though we are affected because our thoughts and words govern our demonstration.*

The unfailing resource is always ready to give. Pour your living words of faith into the omnipresent ethers and you will prosper though all the banks in the world close their doors. Turn the great energy of your thinking upon 'plenty' ideas and you will have plenty regardless of what men about you are saying or doing."

Take heed of the wisdom of Charles Fillmore by "*thinking of plenty of creative ideas.*"

Be open to creative ideas to create multiple streams of income. Think of creative ways to spread your investment in areas where your wealth increases. As the wise saying goes, "Do not place all your eggs in one basket."

Improve your life's work by making time for creative ideas. Innovate, improve and reinvent. Inspired action benefits everyone, not just you!

If you are self-employed, create multiple revenue models for your products and services. Be open to multiple ideas and multiple opportunities, new inventions, new ways of doing things and new applications. When we give birth to new projects, inventions and services, the riches of our country expand and thus, the economy of our country becomes buoyant.

For new creative ideas to unfold for spectacular possibilities, an excellent way to stimulate our creative capacity and excel superlatively in any endeavor is through these methods:

- *Brainstorm, listen and examine every idea. No idea is silly.*
- *Weigh the usefulness of every idea, for every idea is creative; just because it comes from a point of view that is different from yours, doesn't make it silly or useless!*
- *Accept failures as experimentation and lessons.*
- *Intelligently embrace change.*
- *Think of creative ways of doing things.*
- *Develop curiosity and a questioning mental attitude.*
- *Develop multiple alternative creative ideas, solutions, options, responses and contingency plans.*
- *Associate with people of different skills, background and experience. This widens the scope of creative ideas. Do not mete out judgments at the onset.*

What's Your Creative Niche?

The ultimate competitive challenge in creating riches is finding your own creative niche. There is no need to compete; your life is not meant to be a race or a battle. Simply find your talent and gift, work on it, get creative with it, and the riches you desire will come to you.

Do not feel that your talents and ideas are insignificant. Nobody's talents and ideas are insignificant. God has bestowed each of us with unique creative talent and there is a desire for the fruits of that labor.

Do not compare yourself to others, except as incentive to continually improve your skills. Do not strive to be better than others; strive to be the best you can be. There are people who will benefit from your unique style or approach. Honor the divine gifts you have received by expressing them fully and joyfully.

You must never feel or think that resources and opportunities to create riches are being monopolized. There is no need for you to compete for your riches. Escape the rat race of trying to outdo, outbid, out-maneuver or outwit. Instead, dream up a grand endeavor that you are truly passionate about. Use your unique creative talent to benefit your world, the Divine Universe will then step up to help you create whatever is necessary in order to accomplish your goals.

✫ With a smile say:

> *"I am part of the unlimited, creative Divine Universe. I am unique; my ideas are authentic. There is no shortage or lack of resources in our unlimited Divine Universe. I can have what I want when I align myself with the creative consciousness of our Divine Universe."*

CHAPTER **18**

Desire Princely Riches, Nothing Less

"When you affirm big, believe and pray big, big things happen."

Norman Vincent Peale
The Power of Positive Thinking

S*ome* people who have been living in mediocrity do not have big dreams and do not aim high. These people, when faced with something grand and opulent, start protesting:

"This is too magnificent, too grand for me!"
"It is too good for me! I don't deserve it!"

Too many magnificent princely riches are lost to people who feel unworthy and believe that they only deserve mediocrity. They constantly deny themselves the very best because they think there is no way princely riches can be theirs.

If you tell yourself you deserve only meager means and mediocrity, or that you can't have something more and better, then meager and mediocrity is what you most assuredly will get.

When the wealthy walk into a room, they 'own it'. They proclaim their desire for princely riches and they get them. Unfair, you might say, but is it? All they are doing is asserting their right to partake in the super abundance of our Divine Universe. They are affirming that they are part of the prosperous Divine Universe.

A Story of a Widow Who Desired Princely Riches

A female acquaintance of mine, was widowed with three children. Her husband died without leaving any material wealth to his family. And my friend had to work hard to support not only her children but her aged mother as well. She would speak to her relatives and friends of her desire to marry, but not just anyone; she wanted to marry a gentleman of Princely Riches.

Her friends and relatives laughed at her dream, saying no man would marry her because of the huge responsibility. But this friend paid no attention to the negativity of her friends and relatives. Instead, she would pray affirming that her Divine God would bring her a husband that would look after her children and her aged mother. She would also visualize a loving husband taking care of her children and mother, dining in expensive restaurants, wearing the best of clothes, living in a big mansion and driving expensive cars.

She would surround herself with symbols of wealth by visiting expensive car showrooms and going for test drives, stimulating an environment of richness and continuously feeding herself with thoughts and beliefs of luxury as her birthright, and blessing everyone else to have luxuries as well. She would also walk into designer boutiques not to buy, but to window shop. As she walked through the boutiques, she would silently bless the boutiques and its clothes, the staff and the proprietors. She would tell herself that she deserved to wear the designer outfits.

Sometimes, she would take evening walks in expensive neighborhoods and mentally tell herself that she deserved to live in expensive, beautiful homes. She would bless the expensive mansions of the wealthy, their families and their wealth.

In her prayers, she would include mental commands such as:

> *"My birthright is princely riches. I am a royal queen of this Divine Universe. Everyone gives me royal respect. With divine love, my princely riches are flowing to me right now."*

Can you guess what happened?

Within a few months of her prayers for princely riches, she met a rich man who fell in love with her, married her, and provided her and her children and aged mother with all the princely riches of the world.

The moral of this story is that without self-respect, you shut down the entire process of manifestation for princely riches. If you feel unworthy, you attract unworthy things and situations. If you feel disrespect for yourself, you attract disrespect.

Dr. Wayne W. Dyer, in his book *The Power of Intention,* wisely penned a brilliant piece of wisdom, related to the same lines, that says, *"If you disrespect yourself, you are showing contempt for the process of creation."*

You Too Can Have Princely Riches.
It is your birthright!

Adopt the mindset of princely riches. Remove the fallacy that only some people can have princely riches.

Never ever say, "I don't deserve it."

In fact, you deserve all the princely riches of this Divine Universe! You are an offspring of this Divine Universe! You deserve princely riches nothing less.

Spiritual author Deepak Chopra, in his book *Creating Affluence*, says, *"Luxury is our natural state. Adopting luxury as a lifestyle sets the preamble, the preconditions for the flow of wealth."*

Adopt the mindset of luxury. Accept that your desires for the best are divine impulses. Always picture yourself living in luxury. Driving cars nothing less than a Mercedes or Rolls Royce. Travelling in first class or in your own aircraft. Picture yourself dining in 5-star to 7-star restaurants.

Hold your head high, stand tall, and walk the self-confidence of a prosperous person. Project confidence, prosperity, friendliness, trustworthiness, and connect with people by making eye contact and through firm handshakes.

Celebrate your life delighting in beautiful things; it is your birthright!

Prosperity teacher Catherine Ponder, said, *"Just as you absorb the light of the sun and freshness of the air, make it a point to absorb beauty in every form that pleases your soul. As you drink in the beauty of nature; as you revel in the beauty of elegant clothes; as you admire the beauty of fine art, music and literature; as you absorb the beauty of illumined, uplifted thoughts, you are feeding your inner beauty."*

There is nothing too good for you, as you are the rightful heir to all the riches of our Divine Universe. Princely riches are your heritage. Boldly claim them right this instant!

☆ With a smile, say this mantra. Say it with feeling, as our kind and most loving Divine Universe responds to your words with feelings:

"I am blessed and everything comes to me effortlessly. I am a princely child of this Divine Universe and rightful heir to the princely wealth of this Divine Universe. I claim all luxuries.

I claim princely cars, princely homes, a princely career and I have the best of families. My princely riches are endless and inexhaustible. Luxury is my natural state. I am right now receiving all the princely, infinite riches I desire."

CHAPTER 19

The Foundation of All Riches

"Everything around you exists as part of the universal mind, also called God/All—That-Is."

Sanaya Roman
Spiritual Growth

*E*verything that exists in this Divine Universe exists because of our most loving, kind, intelligent, generous and all-mighty Divine God. You can also call it Divine Substance or the Divine Universal Mind. *"All the riches of this Divine Universe are available to everyone."*

Legendary prosperity teacher, Catherine Ponder, in her book *The Dynamic Laws of Prosperity* said, *"God is the source of your supply—not people. Although people, ideas and opportunities are channels of your supply, God is the source because God creates those ideas and opportunities through the 'Law of Mind'. God helps attract the appropriate people and circumstances to you to help expedite those ideas and opportunities through which your good can come to pass."*

How amazingly true!

The real source and supply of all our needs is our loving Divine God. Employers, clients, friends, customers, employees and others are merely instruments through which our loving Divine God, channels all our goods.

Connecting with
The Divine Foundation of Your Riches

Keep your loving Divine God in your mind, in every thought, every act and in whatever endeavor you undertake. Communicate with your Divine God on all your heart's desires. As the spiritual saying goes, "first seek the kingdom of God" as the kingdom of God is the source of your riches. Pour all your heart's desires and needs to your foundation of riches and all of its divine riches will flow to you.

No matter how and when you call upon this most kind, loving and generous power, it will respond to you. All you need is faith and to be open to receiving what you desire.

Be appreciative and thankful for all the ideas that come to your mind. The ideas that come to your mind are given to you by Divine God, so that you put these ideas to work in your affairs. This is why inspiration is so powerful and should never, ever be dismissed. 'Inspired' literally means *the divine spirit within.*

Every time you are inspired to do something fruitful that will have a beneficial effect on everyone, this means you have just received divine guidance! Act on it immediately without any doubt.

Whatever you are undertaking, know that your loving God is with you, guiding you, protecting you, prospering you and teaching you. Do not fear anything. Keep going until you materialize your desire. Due to past conditioning, sometimes old beliefs such as panic, worry about recession and competition may arise in your mind. When this happens,

⭐ With a smile say:

> *"I will not allow thoughts and talk of insufficiency to bother me. These old beliefs are flawed and they do not exist in my world. They have no power over me.*
>
> *My loving Divine God, my divine substance, is my foundation of riches. I am well looked after for my loving God gives abundance to all.*
>
> *My loving God is with me every moment. My loving God is the Divine Provider for all my needs and right now is prospering me with all the riches I desire."*

CHAPTER **20**

Rise to Riches in the Legitimate Plane

> "We ought to get rich if we can by honorable methods,
> and these are the only methods that sweep us quickly
> toward the goal of riches."
>
> Russell H. Conwell
> Acres of Diamonds

*H*ave you ever noticed that some people enjoy super riches for many generations or more, while the riches of others get dissipated without even realizing it?

Why is this so?

What are the flaws of those whose wealth does not last long?

"It is personal integrity."

Acquiring riches without integrity has immense negative consequences. Either the riches will soon disappear or they will weigh upon the soul with a heavy burden of shame and guilt. Those kinds of riches leave in their wake only the unhappy debris of dishonesty and never the joyful and abundant exuberance that legitimate riches bring.

Some people resort to fraud or manipulation to achieve their own goals. It is a misguided attempt to enrich oneself, believing that 'others must lose so that I may win' mentality is the only way to attain wealth or success.

Even such seemingly benign methods such as profiting from the mistakes and ignorance of others, hindering the prosperity or successful progress of others, destroying freedom of creativity and squelching others' desires for advancement, have negative consequences for both the people being harmed, as well as the person who is profiting from these activities.

Legendary prosperity teacher and author James Allen in his popular book *Eight Pillars of Prosperity* says, *"There is no striking a cheap bargain with prosperity. It must be purchased, not only with intelligent labor, but with moral force. As the bubble cannot endure, so the fraud cannot prosper. He makes a feverish spurt in the acquirement of money, and then collapses. Nothing is ever gained, ever can be gained, by fraud. It is but wrested for a time, to be again returned with heavy interest."*

Perfectly said! This Divine Universe is built upon divine spiritual laws and principles, and we are all subject to them.

Riches with Conscience

Creating riches with conscience means having an overriding desire to benefit and enrich everyone, not only yourself, and never at others' expense. Acquiring legitimate riches means you encourage freedom of creativity and help others to succeed and prosper.

It means never profiting from the mistakes or ignorance of others. It means there is no lying, stealing, manipulating or defrauding. It means that the one who causes harm to humans, animals or the environment never attains legitimate riches. "*The desire is for all life to prosper.*"

Wallace D. Wattles in his book, *Science of Getting Rich,* said, "*To be one with the mind of nature is to seek the advancement of all at the expense of none; to seek to get for all what one desires to get for one's self.*" What a brilliant insight!

The more you can take your business or personal endeavors to the legitimate plane, the more prosperity you will attract. There is a divine, golden, eternal law called the 'Law of Cause and Effect'. In other words it means, "*We reap what we sow.*"

In the operation of our daily life's endeavors with one another, we should be fair, just and equitable, ensuring abundance mutually.

We must let go of any fears of lack or scarcity. We must let go of the need for others to lose so that we may win. Adopt a feeling of trust in your loving Divine God, who is the source of all riches and there is no need to attain them by sacrificing integrity or honesty.

Even difficult economic times or times of personal struggle do not warrant dishonorable behavior. While you may profit in the short run, you can be sure that the consequences of your actions will come back to you. Once you realize that, your perception changes and you will never again think about taking the 'low road' to riches.

The Legitimacy of Your Choices

You must accept that every choice you have made has resulted in where you are now. The first step is to become conscious of your choices simply by witnessing your reactions to situations and the choices you make on a daily basis.

Keep in mind that many of your actions and ways of speaking are so ingrained in you that they are subconscious. They are habits, formed by past conditioning. By becoming aware of the way you speak and the things you do, you begin to see that your current situation is indeed a direct result of that subconscious behavior.

The essence of 'legitimate choices' is whether or not the choice, deep down, in your heart and soul, makes you feel good. Does it make you happy?

Some of us have a tendency not to listen to the urgings of our soul. Instead, we look at the current situation and make choices based on our fears of poverty that hinder the acquisition of legitimate riches.

How do you override the conditioned response and make choices that are virtuous and reflect your integrity?

Firstly, listen to your heart! It's more important to listen to your heart than your logical, conditioned mind. Every time you talk yourself into or out of something and have that sneaking suspicion that you're not making the correct choice, you are right!

Every time you say "yes" when you would rather say "no," you end up compromising your happiness. Think about a business. If the business owner believes in protecting the environment, he or she would do so at any cost rather than looking at the 'bottom line' and doing something, however minor, that harms the environment.

Secondly, question yourself! *"Will this choice bring me and those around me happiness?"*

Be aware of what your heart and your gut instinct are telling you. If you are distressed because of your choice, don't make it! In the above example, choosing to spend money on protecting the environment will ultimately benefit everyone and lead to success and happiness.

How do you know whether it is the 'heart' talking or the 'mind' talking?

A simple clue: every time you make a choice that creates happiness, you should experience an immediate physical sense of well-being. Learn to listen to your body when you feel you have a difficult decision to make. The choice you make that results in 'spontaneous right action', the right action at the right moment, is the choice that makes everything feel right; your heart feels good, your body feels light and you just 'know' it.

With a smile, say to yourself:

> *"When I approach life from the perspective of desiring riches, happiness and love for all, then that is what will come back to me. Living life according to the legitimate acquisition of riches is truly joyful, fulfilling and meaningful and will lead me to riches, super riches, effortlessly and spontaneously.*

I will joyfully protect, enhance and support all life of our Divine Universe. I will lovingly take action that benefits others and ensures abundance for all.

I will act with honesty, integrity and in the spirit of service. Safety, social responsibility and sustainability are paramount."

CHAPTER 21

Vow of Riches

"Within you lie all the answers and talents you need to create unlimited abundance for yourself, to have what you need both physically and spiritually in every area of your life. You are a magnificent, powerful person. You can learn to tap into the unlimited abundance of the universe."

Sanaya Roman & Duane Packer
Creating Money

*N*ow that you have read rise to riches. You need to have a personal vow of riches. This personal vow of riches is a powerful creed, or blueprint.

Sign it, and read it often with love and joy and when you put it into practice; you will align with the consciousness of our beautiful Universe.

My Heart's Personal Vow of Riches

I am a magnificent, divine child of this beautiful Divine Universe. I can have whatever I want to have. I can be whatever I desire to be. I am worthy of love and respect.

I am here to experience life joyfully and discover my journey to riches, super riches. I am here to be kind, respect, and honor, cherish, applaud and love myself for what I am. I am here to grow intellectually and spiritually, to express the fullness of life by becoming ever-greater versions of myself.

I will illuminate my Divine Universe with my loving hands, kind words, divine thoughts and intentions, righteous actions and compassionate heart. I will give, share, uplift, and radiate joy, happiness, love, light and peace to all. My connection with everyone and everything is of a spiritual nature. I see divinity in everyone.

I consciously choose all my thoughts to always feel good, joyful and happy. I bring joy to unhappy situations. I nullify all negativities with my higher energy of divine light, love, bliss, joy, peace and harmony.

I remain in a perpetual state of gratitude and humility to my ever-loving, Divine God and God's Divine Universe for all that is in my life and the life of others. I make a commitment right now to always remain in harmony with the consciousness of my loving God.

My responsibility is to expand my talents and use them to create riches for the betterment of everyone. Infinite super riches are my birthright. I deserve the unlimited riches of this beautiful Divine Universe simply because I am the divine child of my Divine God. I live the truth I came to be!

. . . .

Signature

Special Praises, Gratitude and Appreciation

My sincere appreciation and gratitude to the authors of the following books, as they have always inspired me. I thank them for sharing their knowledge and wisdom. This book is enhanced with their words of wisdom and I recommend all my dear readers these books for a richer and happy life.

References and Suggested Reading:

Alvin Toffler, *The Third Wave*. Bantam Books, Bantam Doubleday Dell Publishing Group, Inc. 1990.

Catherine Ponder, *The Dynamic Laws of Prosperity*. Prentice – Hall, Inc, 1962.

Catherine Ponder, Open *Your Mind to Receive*. Unity School of Christianity 1971.

Catherine Ponder, *How to Live a Prosperous Life*. www.self-improvement-ebooks.com 2006.

Christian Larson, *The Path to Roses*. Thomas Y. Crowell Co, New York, 1913.

Charles Fillmore, *Prosper*. Unity Book (Unity School of Christianity), 1994.

Charles Fillmore, *Dynamics for Living*. White Dog Publishing, 1967.

Deepak Chopra, *Creating Affluence*. Amber Allen Publishing and New World Library, 1998.

Deepak Chopra, *Spontaneous Fulfillment of Desire*. Random House, Inc, NY, 2003.

David Hawkins, *Power Vs Force*. Hay House Inc USA, 2002.

Eugene Fersen, *Science of Being*. www.scienceofbeingsecrets.com 1927.

Ester and Jerry Hicks, *The Amazing Power of Deliberate Intention*. Hay House Inc, 2006.

Ester and Jerry Hicks, (The teaching of Abraham) *Money and Law of Attraction*. Hay House Inc, 2008.

Ester and Jerry Hicks, *Ask and It is Given*. (The teaching of Abraham). Hay House Inc, 2005.

Eckhart Tolle, *The Power of Now*. New World Library, USA, 2005.

Eknath Easwaran, *The Upanishads*. Nilgiri Press, Blue Mountain Canada, 2009.

Henry Thomas Hamblin, *Within You is the Power*. Gutenberg USA, 2005 (ebook#7224).

Helen Schucman, *A Course in Miracles*. Foundation or Inner Peace, 1976.

John Kehoe, *Mind Power*. Zoetic Inc, 2010.

James Allen, *Eight Pillars of Prosperity*. Princeton Cambridge Publishing Group, 2010

Joseph Murphy, *The Power of Your Subconscious Mind*. Prentice-Hall, Englewood Cliffs, 1963.

Joseph Murphy, *The Power of Subconscious Mind*. Prentice Hall, 1963.

Lynne McTaggart, *The Intention Experiment*. Free Press, 2007.

Laurence G. Boldt, *Tao of Abundance*. Penguin Group, 1999.

Napolean Hill, *Your Magic Power to be Rich*. Penguin Group (USA) Inc New York, 2007.

Napolean Hill, *Law of Success*. Success Unlimited, 1979.

Sanaya Roman & Duane Packer, *Creating Money*. New World Library, 2008.

Sanaya Roman, *Spiritual Growth*. HJ Kramer Inc USA, 1989.

Sanaya Roman, *Personal Power through Awareness*. HJ Kramer Inc, 1986.

Sarah Ban Breathnach, *Simple Abundance*. Bantam Books, 1997.

Thomas Troward, *Law and the Words. The Edinburgh Lecture Notes*, Gutenberg USA, 1917.

Thomas Troward, *The Hidden Power*. New York, R.M. McBride & Company, 1921.

Russel H. Conwel, *Acres of Diamond*. Wilder Publications. USA, 2007.

Robin Sharma, *The Greatness Guide Book*. Harper Collins Publishers Ltd 2007.

Robin Sharma, *The Greatness Guide Book* Two. Harper Collins Publishers Ltd 2007.

Ryonda Bryne, *The Magic.* Atria Books. Simon & Schuster Inc New York 2012.

Walter C. Lanyon, *Leaves of the Trees.* Elva M. Weidman Peoria, IL.

Wallace D. Wattles, *The Science of Getting Rich.* Best Success Books USA. 1910.

Wayne W. Dye, *The Power of Intention.* Hay House, Inc, 2010.

Notes

Notes

Notes

Notes

Notes